JOHN B. SNOOK

is a professor in the department of religion in
Barnard College of Columbia University in New
York City. He is the author of *Doing Right and
Wrong* and several essays on contemporary re-
ligion.

GOING FURTHER

Life-and-Death Religion in America

JOHN B. SNOOK

A SPECTRUM BOOK

PRENTICE-HALL, INC. ENGLEWOOD CLIFFS, NEW JERSEY

Library of Congress Cataloging in Publication Data

SNOOK, JOHN B
    Going further; life-and-death religion in America.

    (A Spectrum Book)
    Includes bibliographical references.
    1. United States—Religion.   2. Sects—United States.   I. Title.
BR515.S63   200'.973   73–14532
ISBN   0–13–357814–3
ISBN   0–13–357806–2 (pbk.)

10   9   8   7   6   5   4   3   2   1

PRENTICE-HALL INTERNATIONAL, INC. (*London*)
PRENTICE-HALL OF AUSTRALIA PTY. LTD. (*Sydney*)
PRENTICE-HALL OF CANADA LTD. (*Toronto*)
PRENTICE-HALL OF INDIA PRIVATE LIMITED (*New Delhi*)
PRENTICE-HALL OF JAPAN, INC. (*Tokyo*)

Contents

Preface

Any book is a kind of crystallization of many aspects of the writer's experience—reading, reflection, and sharing impressions with others. This is true even when the subject written about is highly technical and the effect of personal factors is at a minimum. In religion, however, how a writer reflects on his own experience is a critical matter, as are the experiences he chooses to examine as a basis for what he says about religion. Is it enough, for example, only to read about a given religious group? Is it enough to talk to members of the group about their experience? If one attends worship with them, can one really catch the essence of what it means to belong? Must one be a believer oneself?

Obviously the last question can't be a requirement for someone who wants to write about a group he doesn't belong to, and there is much to suggest that insiders find it difficult to present their faith fairly because of what it commits them to. But I would argue that it is necessary whenever possible to attend worship, to talk to members of a group, and to try with sympathy to discover what they gain from participation in it.

From the author's point of view, these considerations have a lot to do with a proper approach to the study of religious groups. Students in the field who use this book may be interested in knowing that the approach taken in it is a kind of commentary on the sociological analysis of religious groups in terms of church, denomination, and sect. To the author's mind, these types are of limited usefulness, chiefly because they do not give enough insight into the quality of experience which is the basis for different forms of religious association. For this reason this book works on the basis of a distinction between conventional and unconventional belief, a point whose theoretical connections must be made elsewhere.

At this point it is appropriate only to make note of some aspects of the writer's experience which in retrospect seem particularly important to the impressions presented here. Study with Professor Robert T. Handy of Union Theological Seminary provided an introduction to unconventional Christian groups; Professor Joseph L. Blau of Columbia University pointed the way to similar Jewish groups. The author is grateful to Priscilla Hailes, Minister of Public Information of the Founding Church of Scientology in New York, for the information and experience she provided; to Dennis Helming of Opus Dei; and to Sherwood Wirt of the Billy Graham Evangelical Association. Also, and not least, to a number of students who made important contributions to the work—Bertha Armstead, Perry Berkowitz, Eileen Freeman, Barbara Paris, Catherine Rossbach, Lory Skwerer, and Cynthia Wagner. Finally, the author expresses his gratitude to all those who in one way or another shared their religious experience with him and helped him to whatever degree of understanding these pages demonstrate.

Introduction:
The Importance
of Unconventional Belief

What is happening to religion in America? America is a nation in which many people care very deeply about their faith and about its future in the national life. Whether or not they are regular church-goers, many Americans worry about the present condition of the churches. They read about the decline in church membership, priests leaving the Roman Catholic Church in significant numbers, and a host of difficulties that beset traditional religious institutions. How serious is the situation? Attacks are leveled against the churches not just by unbelievers, but especially by those with good credentials —thinking people, believing people, even clergymen and theologians who declare that "God is dead" and that the familiar institutions have lost their usefulness and are headed for collapse. If even the professionals have lost their nerve, ordinary people may well ask what is left for them to do.

On the basis of such evidence, many a sceptic would predict the end of the religious forms that we have known heretofore. Such a prediction would be nothing new, however, because for centuries in the Western world the decline and fall of religion have been confidently forecast, and people have even begun to express nostalgia for Christendom, or for Israel, on the assumption that both were effectively things of the past. Until now such feelings have been premature. Yet there are, no doubt, many who would say that the end of religion has finally come, and that religion in America is about finished. Do we know enough to say so? If such a prediction is to be trusted, it has to be based on more than superficial evidence. Thus the first step in learning what is happening now is learning how to find evidence good enough on which to base our predictions.

I would argue, however, that even the best of evidence may not give us all the information we need. All predictions, no matter how well supported by facts, are acts of the imagination. Those who make them have to choose between facts that support one explanation and facts that may suggest quite a different one. So where religion in America is concerned, the first step toward an informed prediction is some knowledge of the facts; after that comes imagination. Now when we look to history for our first set of facts, we find that no clear and simple picture emerges. The churches have had both ups and downs. In the recent past the Depression of the thirties was a very bad time for laity and clergy alike, and naturally also for the general feeling in the land about the future of religion. Yet in the years after World War II—the period which shaped the experience of the majority of living Americans—a completely different impression prevailed. Religion made news that on the whole was good. As the suburbs grew, there was a prodigious increase in the construction of houses of worship. Attendance rose, so that toward the end of the fifties the Gallup Poll showed that very close to half of the adults in the country attended weekly at least one service of worship.[1] Correspondingly, people generally believed that religion was gaining in influence. In some significant ways it was, but it would certainly have been wrong to make any long-range predictions on the basis of those statistics, just as it would have been wrong to draw final conclusions from the facts of the thirties.

In a similar way, the trends of the sixties ought not to lead us to an altogether pessimistic view of the state of religion in America in the seventies and in the decades to come. In the sixties the direction that organized religion was taking, of course, was the reverse of what had been true only a few years before. Church attendance, though still impressive by the standards of most European countries, began to drop off slowly but perceptibly, and year after year fewer and fewer people believed that religion was increasing its influence. Since most Americans are members of religious organizations, what this indicated was a serious loss of morale within institutions long

1. See Gallup Opinion Index, "Special Report on Religion," February 1969.

established in American life, the denominations that in past years gathered their congregations and raised their ridgepoles in all the towns of the land.

On the other hand, though many people have offered reasons for the change, it is really very difficult to know why it took place. It is undoubtedly true, for example, that some people have taken leave of their religious group because they believed it did not do enough in terms of some of the great social issues of the sixties—the civil rights movement and the movement against American involvement in Southeast Asia. For these people the church has not been relevant enough to present-day conditions. The trouble is that we do not have evidence good enough to justify such an interpretation of the change in every case. It is likely that other people have behaved in just the opposite way, leaving a church because it has seemed too involved in the events of the day, too neglectful of its obligation to help people renew themselves spiritually.

One extremely important factor in the religious situation of the sixties was the crisis in the Roman Catholic Church. Many changes have been made in its ancient traditions, with the intention of bringing it more closely in touch with the point of view of modern man. Yet there is some evidence that such changes have led to confusion and doubt for many of the faithful, rather than to the grateful response and deeper participation that had been expected. It is difficult, therefore, to predict the future of the largest single religious group in this country.

If we ought not to extend too far into the future the trends of the sixties and seventies, and if we cannot depend too much on the current mood of churchgoing people and the reasons given for their loss of confidence in the future of religion, is there any source of information that can give us a better means of prediction? If our past history is a reliable guide—and despite many statements to the contrary, there are reasons to believe that it can be relied on—the seed of what is to come to maturity in American religion is not planted in the places where we have just been looking. Again and again in our past, as a matter of fact, the force behind religious change has come from unexpected origins—not so much from the mainstream as from the tributaries, the backwaters, or the waters from the cracks in old dams no longer sound. New emphases in faith, even new gospels, and the ardent quests of people unsatisfied with what the older institutions were able to do for them have been the stimuli for groups that later became the established denominations, firmly fixed in the conventional fabric of everyday life in America.

What if we look, then, at the unconventional religions in America? Here any reading of the popular media gives the impression of an almost tropical abundance of growth, rather than the appearance of disillusionment and decline. Among young people there seems to be a virtual explosion of interest in and attachment to a host of different religious groups. There are the Jesus Freaks and the Jews for Jesus, the religious communes, and any number of groups responding to various elements in the religious traditions of India and Japan. Among older people the situation is not altogether different from that of the young. Again and again one sees evidence that not all religious groups by any means are part of the general picture of demoralization and decline.

This leads us to ask which groups have stood out against the major trend. Many of the groups that have prospered are those not large enough to affect the totals in the regular statistics, either because they are individually not very large or because they do not report their membership to the people who collect the figures. There is reason to think that the total number of people involved in all such groups taken collectively is impressive. In addition, among the more traditional groups, the ones that seem to have done best, at least within the Protestant community, are those that have stood for something clear and positive, however old-fashioned it seemed to the sophisticated. The "old-time religion" draws people in new ways but with little if any loss of the power of the old revivals. The preacher may wear a microphone in his lapel, speak through amplifiers, and be backed up by musicians using the latest electronic equipment, but the basic appeal is old and effective. People are moved, and they respond.

There are many obvious differences between the groups of old-time believers, standing four-square behind a version of the faith that most of their fellow believers have given up long ago, and the groups whose faith is self-consciously new and contemporary. The evangelist Oral Roberts, for example, built a remarkable career on works of healing by the power of prayer, and he is the center of a network of friendships and associations of a quite traditional kind. Scientology, on the other hand, though it is also built on a program of healing and spiritual regeneration, and though it is very much the creation of another remarkable personality, makes its way by giving people something new, a method of self-improvement and regeneration anchored in the language of science and utilizing, not prayer, but a therapy administered with the help of a machine. In the Roman Catholic world, the more avant-garde believers bind themselves to experimental forms of worship and to programs of revolutionary social reform, while others display a passionate commitment to the beauties of the Latin text of the Mass, now rarely used, and to obligations such as fasting on Friday, which no longer are officially required. Among Jews, similarly, the most dynamic groups of believers seem to be those on either edge of the community—people who make a total commitment to the old faith and its practice, on the one hand, and other people who are devoting much of their energy to reinterpreting Judaism in order to make it relevant to the conditions of modern life.

In other words, among all the major religious traditions of this country within the past few years, growth seems to be taking place not at the center but at the edges. This means not only that attention has been captured by the new and the innovative, but also that new life has been breathed into the older forms that modern ways seemed to have doomed.

Can we make sense out of tendencies seemingly so contrary? It is the contention of this book that we can, and that the attempt to do so teaches much of value about the present and future realities of religion in American society or, to go a step further, in any other society as well.

CONVENTIONAL AND UNCONVENTIONAL RELIGION

To suggest how this may be, we ask the reader to take seriously the image of the center and the edges that was just discussed. The things that are happening at opposite edges of the same body may be quite different when compared with each other, but they are similar in their basic location with regard to the central, the normal, the expected. From this point of view there are two basic kinds of religious expression, the "conventional" and the "unconventional." There is the religion that people take for granted and make a familiar part of their lives, in which they participate and follow almost unquestioningly, or at least without considering that it must drive them into new ways of thinking, feeling, and behaving; and there is the religion that will not leave them alone, that requires them to ignore the everyday world and thrust themselves into a world differently understood and differently organized. This may be a novel religious vision or an ancient one. Either may take you far from the ordinary world.

Neither kind of religion—conventional or unconventional—is necessarily better or worse than the other, since to a considerable degree the vitality of either depends on the conditions of the times and the personalities who practice it. But again and again it has happened that neither kind of believer has felt comfortable in the presence of the other; their opposition has generated endless religious conflict and change. The postwar years in America were years of progress and optimism; the religious expression of this era of positive thinking was solid growth of the institutions of conventional religion, as we have already noted. People came to feel that joining a church or synagogue was as natural as buying a house or being visited by the "welcome wagon" in a new community. The book that caught the essence of these developments perhaps more than any other was Will Herberg's *Protestant-Catholic-Jew*.[2] Herberg here suggested that membership in any of these three great traditions had come to be accepted as part of the American way of life, which he felt was the true religion of the people of America. At the same time, with a prophet's spirit he criticized the ignorance and the complacency that characterized the involvement of most Americans in their religious institutions. Their ignorance, however, did not mean that church members were not serious about religion as they understood it. I suspect that what Herberg caught so well was the spirit of a time in which conventional religion prevailed, and the prophet and the saint seemed more than a little ridiculous.

Times change, and in the sixties the circle revolved until the old optimism and progress had been replaced by gloom; but in such circumstances the other kind of religion—the unconventional— emerged as the more attractive of the two for many people. Times became more troubled, and it may be that at such times traditional institutions can satisfy no one. People of a conventional turn of mind are upset because their church does not protect them against change. On the other hand, people with unconventional beliefs either attempt to pressure others into radically new commitments or seek a group where they think religion is taken more seriously. As we have suggested, this may be a conservative group, one that from the standpoint of historical development seems very much a reactionary throwback. Or it may be a radically new development. Yet either outcome may be seen as a product of essentially the same dynamism, the motive that rejects the conventional in religion and offers scope for something more.

In order to clarify these differences, let us explore further some of the implications of the distinction between conventional and unconventional religion. "Unconventional believers" is, after all, an

---

2. Will Herberg, *Protestant-Catholic-Jew* (Garden City, N. Y.: Doubleday and Company, Inc., 1955 and 1960).

ambiguous term, and the reader may well have wondered whether it refers to people or to the groups to which they belong. As we have already suggested, it has to do fundamentally with the religious experience of individuals. What are such people like? Quite simply, they are people who believe and practice their faith in ways that they recognize as out of the ordinary. For religious reasons they set themselves apart from other people. This does not necessarily mean that they are overly emotional, unstable, or even unusually pious, because there are many ways in which this sense of religious apartness may be expressed. A believer may be convinced in a rational and wholly unemotional way that he has the truth, or he may have decided that the morality of the Sermon on the Mount, for example, needs to be obeyed to the letter. It should be recognized that often it is the unconventional believers whose arguments make the better case. They are the ones who take seriously the teachings of their faith and try to obey its injunctions in all their fullness.

As a rule, of course, unconventional believers are more emotionally involved in their faith than conventional believers. Some are horrified by the abyss between religious promises and their fulfillment, and it is they who feel the agony in the terrible questions about God's justice and His willingness to show mercy to all His creatures. For such unconventional believers, religion tends to become every day a matter of immediate life and death. Like Jacob, they wrestle with angels and refuse to let go until they receive a blessing. Or like Martin Luther, they cannot be obedient children of the church until they know that God has been gracious personally to them. Or like Blaise Pascal, the great French mathematician and religious thinker of the seventeenth century, they see faith as the ultimate wager, a necessary gamble against the possibility that there is no final meaning in life. Or like any number of individuals, both celebrated and unsung, who have been touched by the sense that religious meaning is that which is of final importance, the unconventional believers of our time set themselves on a spiritual journey that they expect will end far away from the place of its beginning.

Probably it is impossible for such pilgrimages ever to be perfectly organized, because so much is at stake for the individuals involved in them. But they always have a social dimension, in the sense that those who set out on a journey look for guides and companions along the way—guides in people who have gone that way before and companions who may intensify the sense of achievement and fulfillment by their own rejoicing or mitigate the pain by sharing it. Thus our first basic point is that religious experience affects people differently, and that there is such a marked difference between the responses people make to it that they can be divided into two classes, called conventional and unconventional believers. Our second basic point is that the religious groups they belong to will reflect the difference and either offer people scope for both kinds of expression or confine them to only one. It is at the point of connection between individual and group expressions that we must consider other factors if we are to gain some clear sense of what is happening to religion in America today.

On the group, or social, level, the major issue is whether conventional and unconventional believers can be accommodated within the same religious organization. The answer to this, in turn, depends on the relation between religious institutions and the political institutions of the society in which the religion is practiced. In general, most societies have accepted the coexistence of the two kinds of religious expression as a matter of course. In simple traditional societies, for example, where religion is taken for granted as the warp of the social fabric, the unconventional believer becomes a specialist, a kind of expert consultant in the life of the spirit to whom people go for healing or knowledge of the mysteries of the spiritual world. Such a person will also find companions or colleagues, and the result is the formation or perpetuation of groups of experts. These may be formal or informal groups. On the informal side one good example of such a group in contemporary times can be found in Carlos Castaneda's description of the "man of knowledge," the expert in psychedelic herbs who knows how to interpret the events of a spiritual journey.[3] He is one of a group of men well known to each other by virtue of their common possession of spiritual powers. On occasion they meet together to share the sacred smoke, but they do not do so regularly, and each man's efforts are the result of the solitary discipline of gathering the plants that put him in touch with his personal guardian.

Where society and religion are more highly organized, but still traditional, there are groups of monks, priests, nuns, mystics, or learned interpreters of the religious law. Sometimes they too function primarily as individuals, offering themselves to laypeople as experts in knowledge or practices that require a course of formal

3. Carlos Castaneda was trained as an anthropologist and has written provocatively about how his experiences with a Mexican Indian sorcerer whom he calls "Don Juan" made him raise serious questions about the limitations of rational and scientific knowledge in the face of spiritual realities. Four books on this encounter are projected, of which the first two are already available in inexpensive paperback editions. They are: *The Teachings of Don Juan: a Yaqui Way of Knowledge* (New York: Ballantine Books, 1969) and *A Separate Reality* (New York: Pocket Books, 1972).

training. Even under such conditions, however, they often act for each other as well, for example as rabbis do when they gather in meetings of rabbinical associations or sit together at the feet of some of the legendary masters of the law. More than this, of course, many such religious specialists are organized into formal groups in which their religious zeal is channeled and cultivated by communal activities—by labor in a holy cause, by praying or chanting, or by the ecstasy of exhaustion in the sacred dance.

The point is that while such groups are certainly unconventional believers in one sense—deliberately organized to give the opportunity for unusually intense religious experience and participation—they are part of the accepted religious system and recognized as appropriate gathering places only for some people, not for all, or for ordinary people only under certain special circumstances. Thus in the Roman Catholic Church only men can be priests, and only men who have been selected out of the general population of the faithful and subjected to a long and rigorous period of training. Women may qualify as nuns, but they cannot become priests. There are different degrees of qualification and grouping even within these ranks, for some priests and nuns work among laypeople, while others join what are called cloistered orders, groups isolated from the everyday world in communities in which silence and particularly intense spiritual discipline are the rule. Monasticism in the older of the two main Buddhist traditions has a rather different rationale, however. Here it is everyone's obligation to become a monk, but not forever. Men may undertake the discipline for a few months, or for life, depending on their motivation and their aptitude for the monastic regimen. The variety of such possibilities depends on the particular traditions of faith and practice that have been established among the adherents of particular faiths.

THE AMERICAN SITUATION

The situation familiar to most Americans is considerably different from the preceding, though it is a situation that may become general in all industrialized countries that allow religious intentions to be freely exercised by their people. Historically it was of fundamental importance for Americans that Protestantism tried to do away with different degrees of religious qualification among people. This is what is meant in practice by Martin Luther's doctrine of the priesthood of all believers. Everyone is equally qualified and equally obligated, and, at least in theory, no one, not even the

clergyman, can be regarded as living a more religious life than anyone else just by virtue of his position in the church. Everyone is
expected to be a religious specialist. Originally these ideas were developed within the frame of reference of a traditional religious
system of the sort we have just described, but the actual outcome
was quite different, especially in America. During the Reformation
era the states of what is now Germany, along with the nations of Europe, as a rule stayed reasonably close to the old ideal by founding
national or territorial churches that included all their citizens. Such
arrangements were possible in America during the colonial period
only in particular areas like Massachusetts Bay or the Roman
Catholic colony of Maryland. As the nation developed its common
life, it became less and less practical to think of setting up a single
church for all, an established national church under which both
conventional and unconventional believers had to expect to keep a
place for one another.

What Paul Tillich called the "Protestant principle," as a principle
of organization was bound to run into difficulty, since there are
legitimate differences in the intensity of response that any two people have to what is presented to them as religious truth. In theory
they were supposed to be alike, but in practice they were different,
and they tended in each case to want to find others like themselves
and join with them in a group suited to their needs.

The process of selection has naturally resulted in a wide variety
of responses both conventional and unconventional. Some fall pretty
close to the traditional sense of the church as a genuinely communal
religious institution. The tightly knit ethnic groups in America provide many appropriate examples. There are the various Orthodox
churches—Greek, Russian, Albanian, to mention a few—for which
membership in the community is a sign of membership in the
church. In such churches the unconventional believers can find
many different possibilities for the expression of their zeal. Something similar can be said for the Jewish community, especially for
the Orthodox part of it, though on the other hand the division of
Judaism into three subgroups—Orthodox, Conservative, and Reform—also shows a response characteristic of the development of the
typically American religious group. Other examples of groups that
have functioned as regional or ethnic subgroups are the Lutheran
churches, which have only recently ceased to be divided along lines
set by the languages of their German and Scandinavian origins.

It is not necessary for a communal religious group to be bound by
ethnic ties or a common language, however. Probably the most
important example of such a group that is not based on natural

relationships of birth is the Church of Jesus Christ of Latter-Day Saints, more commonly referred to as the Mormon Church. As we shall see, it retains many of the characteristics of a group of unconventional believers, which it was at its founding, but it is significant that present-day Mormons put a great deal of stress on family ties, notably on ties created by ceremonies to which only church members in good standing can be admitted. Mormons consider themselves descendants of the ancient Israelites and thus the true family of God in the New World of America. They tried very hard to construct a kind of traditional religious group, within which several different religious options are possible, even for ordinary people; to a considerable degree they have succeeded, largely because they dominate the religious life of Utah and parts of surrounding states.

CONVENTIONAL AND UNCONVENTIONAL GROUPS

The overall importance of the groups just mentioned needs to be kept in mind in drawing the following picture—that of a religious scene in which the differences between conventional and unconventional believers become the basis for separate and distinct religious groups that exist side by side among basically similar people. Such a description is necessary to an understanding of the religious groups located in the mainstream of the tradition of American religious life. Historically, these are the groups derived from English origins, particularly from the earnest idealism of the Puritans, who began to disturb the Church of England in the days of the first Queen Elizabeth and who not only played a major role in shaping that church in subsequent years but also founded the Presbyterian, Congregational, and Baptist churches, inspired by their writings the formation of the Methodist Church, and provided the context in which revival methods developed. They did all this, and more, in their restless search for the form of the true Church. The groups they founded were unconventional ones at the start but in the intervening years have become the conventional churches of Protestant America. This change in turn has created the need for still other groups to accommodate the unconventional impulse.

As we said previously, it is the unconventional believers who usually have the more convincing argument as to how religion should be lived. Thus no one is likely to set out to found a conventional religious group. Instead, someone with the Puritan's restless soul—the prophets, Jesus, Gautama the Buddha, or any of the great and not-so-great founders of groups devoted to new forms of religious expression—will criticize the shortcomings of existing forms and either institute the new or make something new necessary. Like all religious groups, however, any such groups that persist until a new generation grows up within them become churches in which conventional and unconventional religious interests inevitably exist side by side, among different people and perhaps also within the same individual at different moments of his life. The groups may then become ideological battlegrounds for those who feel it necessary to renew and restore the discipline that accompanied the old enthusiasm and those who are perhaps content with the form of the old without its substance. If the disagreement comes to overt conflict, it is difficult to know what factors determine the outcome. Sometimes it makes a difference that group members recruited from among the poor and downtrodden achieve more comfortable ways of life and become more conventional in their religious practice, but that is not always the case. Some groups retain the dynamism that marks the religious commitment of unconventional believers, but others do not.

One can hardly overemphasize the difference it has made in our religious history that so many Americans who were unconventional believers have taken it for granted that the religious groups to which they belonged could rightly be expected to embody a righteousness equal to their own. We have expected a lot of our religious institutions, but the crucial point is that if we were seriously dissatisfied with the ones we already knew, our response was not to seek out special roles within them—according to the Protestant principle none is really justified—but instead we responded by looking for one that was closer to the ideal, or could be moved that way. If no such group offered itself, it was possible here, certainly more possible here than in most other places, to found a new and unconventional group. The "first vision" of Joseph Smith, for example, had as its central theme the question in Smith's mind as to which church he should join.[4] The figure of Christ answered that existing churches were all wrong, and that Smith should join none of them. Like many other religiously creative individuals in our history, Smith took this advice as a mandate to become "prophet, seer, and revelator" of a new church. His followers had to be aware

4. For an official account of the first vision, see the extract from *The History of Joseph Smith, the Prophet* printed in *The Pearl of Great Price,* published by The Church of Jesus Christ of Latter-Day Saints, p. 48. See also James B. Allen, "The Significance of Joseph Smith's 'First Vision' in Mormon Thought," *Dialogue* I, 3 (Autumn 1966), 29–45.

that what was offered to them, and what was asked of them, was distinctly out of the ordinary. They were, in other words, unconventional believers in a group of unconventional believers.

Is this still true? Can it be said that the Mormon Church is still located at the growing edge of religious movement in this country? It is much easier to answer from the standpoint of origins than from the standpoint of the present situation, because the Mormon faith, though still unusual in many respects, is much less controversial than it was a century ago. But the question is important if the unconventional believer holds the key to present and future developments in American religion. The fact is that our present religious situation is in many ways a living museum built by the unconventional believers of former times. Thus the Congregationalists descend from ardent Puritans, who felt they could build a truer church in New England than the one they knew in the old country, the Baptists from brave spirits who found the Puritans' attitude too confining in many respects, the Methodists from a later episode in much the same scenario, and many a more recent group from the leadership of individuals who felt that there was too great a contrast between what these evangelical churches preached, once they were well established, and what they had actually become.

As a rule, unconventional believers argue that their old churches have become conventional. Such a case has often been made with great passion, but that does not make it true. One purpose of this book is to show that there is often a place for unconventional believers in groups that may seem to have lost their fervor. Another purpose is to examine a sampling of groups of unconventional believers founded in previous times to see whether they are still as lively, and therefore as important, as they once were.

One point to reemphasize here is that while groups of unconventional believers can hold to the substance of their original character only by making clear, both to themselves and to others, that they are different from conventional believers, it is not enough to define themselves simply as opponents of older faiths. They must also have a positive reason for being. One of the conditions of the American situation is that such groups have become specialists in various aspects of religious faith and practice in order to define their identity. Sometimes a point of doctrine is the basis of their distinctiveness. The Seventh-day Adventists are so named because they believe strongly in the early second coming, or advent, of Christ to judge the world and usher in the millennium, and also because they believe that the sabbath, or Saturday, is the day on which the Lord should be worshiped. These beliefs certainly do not sum up what it means to be an Adventist, but they do show how important points of doctrine can be in the formation of a well-established group.

In other groups, however, it is not a point of doctrine that matters, but some other distinguishing emphasis that may inform the life of the group in rather different ways. If it is correct in general to say that salvation in some sense is the goal of all Christian efforts, it is equally true that salvation is not always defined by points of doctrine. Health has been for many people a primary goal of their religious striving. In the history of the Roman Catholic Church this motive has given rise to a host of pilgrimage centers, grottoes, and shrines like Lourdes or Ste. Anne de Beaupré. In Protestant America the more characteristic response to this need has been the health-centered religious group. Healing has been important to the Seventh-day Adventists, but it is done by conventional medical means as an aspect of their missionary and millennial concern. In groups which heal by exclusively religious means, health may move to a more central place, as, for example, in the early work of an evangelist like Oral Roberts, in Christian Science and, more recently, the Church of Scientology.

Other concerns are central in other groups of unconventional believers. Groups among the poor have promised prosperity and dignity in this world and the next. One may recall the extraordinary figure of Father Divine in this regard. In times of heightened racial tension the quality of a particular racial heritage has been given religious value in certain unconventional groups. Thus the Black Muslims have been important on the American religious scene for their belief that black people are superior to whites, and what is called "Black Theology" has given rise to a church called the Shrine of the Black Madonna.

The choice of such emphases often seems arbitrary, especially when the groups that were founded on them live on in times when it is unlikely that a choice like theirs would be made again. Thus the Salvation Army, a name chosen in 1878 to define the evangelistic efforts of William Booth in London, was dedicated to the warfare against the evils of poverty in an urban slum. Its members still don their uniforms and draw recruits to their efforts. Moreover, one would not predict an early end to the army's existence, but it is safe to say that the particular appeal it has had is now shared by a host of secular social agencies; hence it is unlikely that such a group would succeed in establishing itself in the contemporary world, even if the army relinquished the field to others. No new group would be able to link social concerns to evangelism in the same way as before. It does make sense, therefore, to suggest that in the light of history, many groups of unconventional believers came into exist- ence in response to obvious needs that were not being met, or at least not widely enough, by the groups available at the time.

CONTEMPORARY NEEDS

Can we say with any confidence what kinds of needs are giving rise to the unconventional religious groups of our own times, or point out which groups are really typical of these concerns? Despite what has just been said, we need to be careful about making general state- ments in answer to such questions, because individuals who possess deeply felt religious convictions are often enabled to move others in unexpected ways. It is possible, for instance, to find examples of a modern religious response to urban poverty. One of the most im- pressive leaders of an unconventional religious group in recent times is Dorothy Day, a former journalist and a convert to Roman Catholicism. She was moved equally by socialist criticism of the economic order and by the ancient motive of Christian charity to publish a newspaper called *The Catholic Worker* and to minister directly to alcoholics and derelicts from the Bowery in New York City and elsewhere. Similarly, one would hardly expect revival evangelism to be vigorous in an age of affluence and advanced tech- nology, yet in many ways it seems to be flourishing as an expression of widespread religious interest. To recognize such facts leads us at the very least to use general expectations about religion, much as a scientist uses hypotheses—as suggestions that make provisional sense of facts already known and that are then tested by being applied to matters not yet explained. Educated guesses may help us explain things that seemed puzzling before, but they will not explain every- thing, and we must be ready to be surprised by realities that will move us to new and better attempts at explanation.

Two assumptions have guided the choice of evidence presented in this book. The first is that religion when taken seriously makes people discontented with conventional responses to everyday con- cerns, including their everyday religious responses. Thus new growth can begin in conventional groups as well as in those dedi- cated to an unconventional vision. The second, on the other hand, is that new groups which form in a particular historical period some- how reflect the period's special concerns.

Which concerns are reflected in the unconventional religious groups of our contemporary world? One seems very conspicuous. It is what might be called a hunger for deep personal experience. It is the counterpart in religion to the enormous effect of modern psychological study and speculation on our thinking about ourselves. One of its effects is to make innovations in religious doctrine seem less important than they used to be. What one author calls "the pursuit of the millennium," [5] for example, is less likely to provide the dynamism for unconventional belief than would have been the case a century ago. There are, to be sure, groups that make flying saucers vehicles of religious belief, but it is hard to imagine a recurrence of the widespread excitement generated when William Miller, on the basis of devoted study of the Bible, predicted that the second coming of Christ would take place in 1844.

In our time what moves people more frequently is the psychological dynamic behind millennialism; this is the desire to find a haven beyond the limits of everyday feelings, to find a group of people who will support us, allow our deepest feelings to be expressed, and vindicate our sense of our own worth in a world that seems to care only about appearances. Despite the decline of many religious institutions, this dynamic tendency often finds a way to expression in existing organizations. In some cases the people involved seem to feel that new kinds of relationships are necessary, and so the result is a new kind of religious group. For others, by contrast, the effort goes into giving life to older religious forms. An example of the first kind of innovative group would be the emergence among clergy and laity of many denominational churches of experimental forms of worship or of so-called "encounter groups," modeled after developments long established in the field of psychotherapy. The aim of group encounters is "consciousness raising" or, to use another phrase that sounds different but means approximately the same thing, deeper self-understanding attained through conversation that disregards convention to focus on the feelings people have for others in the group, as well as feelings they have about themselves. There is, to be sure, nothing essentially religious about such groups, but in a church setting they can be described in Biblical or theological language, and they can therefore be very helpful to many people in ways which they consider religious. Encounter groups in churches are therefore a significant form of unconventional religious group within the meaning of our definition, but since they do not have a specifically religious reason for being, they are unlikely to become

5. Norman Cohn, *The Pursuit of the Millennium* (New York: Harper and Row, Publishers, Inc., 1961).

anything like a new church or denomination. Instead, they may well continue to generate a spirit of renewal within the denominational churches.

More interesting in many ways to the student of religion today is the other kind of church-related but experience-oriented group, the group that brings people to a deeper level of feeling down traditional religious pathways by way of old religious images. The religious images in this case are not orthodox doctrinal formulations—images of truth used to protect basically conservative people against change—but active images of movement and change, pointing to the living presence of a spirit that tends to get lost when belief is too closely defined by church authorities. In Christian churches these groups are variously called "pentecostal" or "charismatic renewal" groups. The former term is more usually applied to meetings under Protestant auspices, the latter to Catholic ones, though both are somewhat loosely used. These are not long-established denominational groups of the Holiness tradition of Protestantism. They are predominantly new local prayer groups that have become part of information networks and that tell interested individuals where they can meet with people who, like them, want to find worship meetings in which the "gifts of the spirit" are given through prayer, preaching, and "speaking in tongues." It is certainly noteworthy that such groups are alive among middle-class people, not simply among the poor and uneducated. And it is also noteworthy that similar examples can be found among Jews, as will be shown below.

THE PERSONAL DIMENSION

To describe in so summary a way some of the available options for expression of the unconventional religious impulse is not really to show how strongly many people feel about the need for them. Later chapters will remedy this deficiency in part by examining several groups in some detail and allowing them to stand for the whole diverse number. But it is important at this point to give the reader an example of a thoroughly contemporary religious longing that cannot be met in any of the traditional ways. It is appropriate to choose a young person's vision, because the "youth culture," an unfortunate term that puts into one category a variety of responses no less rich and varied than the religious strivings of former times, has in our time been unusually critical of the traditional options and as a result has generated many unconventional religious movements, some of them very old-fashioned and conservative but others self-consciously new.

Conspicuous in the youth culture has been the ready availability and widespread use of drugs. Many people have deplored their use, and some have celebrated them as liberating. The drug experience has obviously had profound consequences for many individuals and families; it has created if not a new social problem at least one broader in scale and therefore more serious than those we have had to face before. No matter what one's feelings are about how the problem should be dealt with, it is not one that can readily be ignored. Even people who are most avidly in favor of a more liberal attitude will acknowledge that drugs can easily be abused, and that the drug experience, no matter what its beauty, can be and often is terrifying. Drug use can serve as an avenue to what the user regards as a religious experience of peculiar intensity. It is certainly no endorsement of drug use to say this but simply a recognition of the fact that many times it has happened so. It is also an admission that many young people today have journeyed further into their mental and perhaps spiritual depths than young people used to do.

Here is what it is like to take such a spiritual journey. The worst of it can be like a case of severe mental illness. One college student described this aspect of the experience as "an excruciating removal from life to some antilife, a hell. I have to restrain myself from describing its horror—like the whole drug experience, you can have no conception of the events and feelings until you do it yourself." Despite the terror it can cause, this "psychotic" type of reaction does not have to be entirely negative in its effects, for the student went on to write that "perhaps my first 'religious' feeling was the discovery in myself of that innermost will to live, that strength which kept 'me' 'myself,' which overcame hell if you will. At that time, alone and without my body in the horrendous antiworld, there was *one* positive thing left and it was something inside of me, *it was me,* and it was Something. It was my soul, it was my life, it was me . . . As a result of this total destruction of my life down to this last point, my essence, I felt I could begin to construct it again, reshape it from the beginning."

In many ways what happened to this student followed the typical course of a religious conversion. She experiences the drug "trip" as a kind of purgation, almost as she might feel absolved after confessing a sin. But there is a more concrete, bodily reference. "I felt that my body had been wholly cleaned and that I could not pollute it.

In spite of periodic infractions, I still maintain a carefully balanced 'health food' diet. . . . This concern for natural, clean food goes along with an awareness of the wonderful beauty of the human body and a respect for its delicately awesome mechanism. When I was a child, I was taught that God gave me the gift of life, but somehow I had never been taught to love my body. In fact, I was taught to hide it, and when I began to mature sexually, I was taught to deny it. The human body is 'God's most beautiful creation,' or Something's most beautiful creation—such an astounding arrangement of living cells—and it *feels* so good! I took to watching people's bodies playing in Central Park, rushing into subways; it was a sort of worship service of what 'God' had wrought. Just performing everyday life functions became for me a celebration of life." She reaches a kind of spiritual rock bottom, and she is purged. Her existence becomes regenerated into a joyous affirmation of life that is at once naïve and knowing. She reports that she no longer makes these psychedelic journeys, being troubled by some of their effects on her mental state and feeling in any case that they have given her all that they could. They retain an importance much like the religious experience of being "born again," but they are so different that she has to put "God" in quotation marks, and her behavior is directed by conventions not at all the same as those of traditional Christian morality.

Whatever its dissimilarity to most American traditions, this experience qualifies as an important form of unconventional believing by virtue of a deeply spiritual quality and an absolute authenticity of perception. Under the influence of the psychoactive drug LSD "the often gorgeous heightening of sensory stimulation can act as an organ and stained-glass windows act in a church service," but the effect is particularly personal: "I remember one spring day in Central Park suddenly becoming aware that everything around me was alive, that the silent forsythia with me there was my sister, that she and the immense black-backed rocks welling up out of the earth, the dead leaves, the single one-inch blades of grass, the rigid clump of buildings arranged patiently at the south side of the park, the bird I could hear but couldn't see, the undiscernible mass of children playing at the other side of the lake, and I were all of the same 'life force' that goes on and on and on.

"In an instant I lost all fear and apprehension of dying, for I *saw* that matter is neither created nor destroyed, it merely changes form or state. I looked forward to the time/un-time when my life force (that same thing I found at the bottom of me during the psychotic experience) would be a breeze, a tree, a flower, a sound, a color. I felt the being of every man that has lived—I felt that I, myself, was a *part* of life. Does this sound absurd? For the first time in my life *I had an identity*. The ultimate security of that feeling of oneness is still my cradle; I recall that overwhelming sense of having an eternal part in life whenever things 'get shaky' in 'this world.' "

What emerges from these words is a feeling very like what the psychoanalyst Erik Erikson speaks of as "basic trust," a feeling of ultimate security that the fortunate derive from a fundamentally loving relation with parents in infancy or, later on, from their religion. The problem is that conventional religion often fails to communicate such trust, and many people feel they must seek it elsewhere.

What this student writes is a good example of the ardor of experience to which unconventional religion may reach. It also suggests some of the reasons why certain contemporary forms of unconventional religion are taking people much farther from the conventional in religion than all but the most extreme sectarian groups used to do. Many of us have become, as it were, ravenous for experience of the inner life, especially because it has become so easy and acceptable in many quarters to feel that we only live once, and that we owe ourselves the full range of pleasure and every variety of experience. "The recent fascination with psychoactive drugs," writes the same student, "has occurred in an inverse relationship to the decrease in concern for traditional, institutionalized religion. As traditional ritual and the Puritan ethic are less important to us, we seek a more earthy, honest means of 'religious' experience and form of expression. I believe that our over-exercised minds have cancelled out this old ritual in favor of celebration, or release, or expression of our nonrational selves in a more unstructured, uninhibited way." Most significantly, perhaps, "this new way is a back-to-the-roots way, an anti-intellectual way, and, as can be expected in the evolution of religion, it is highly individualized if not wholly so."

In other words, much of the current interest in religion is highly personal among the many young people who are totally uninterested in familiar religious traditions except as they furnish ideas for meditation and individual guidance, and occasionally for visionary communal efforts. This turning inward helps explain why there has been a considerable growth of interest in Hindu and Buddhist ideas and images, as well as in the mystical Sufi tradition of Islam. Insofar as these interests have engendered new groups of unconventional believers, they make up a part of the general subject matter of this book, but since they have been the subject of several other recent works, they cannot be given more than the present brief mention.[6] Nevertheless, the reader should keep them in mind when trying to imagine the whole range of possibilities for unconventional believers in contemporary America.

To summarize, differences in the quality and intensity of religious experience divide people into two general groups, which we are calling conventional and unconventional believers. These differences generate in every cultural situation the need for different forms of religious expression, and a kind of restless sense of difference between the people who follow one path or the other. In situations where religion is established as a single institution involving an entire social group, it tends to be taken for granted that these religious differences will be given scope within the limits of the group. There are many groups in America that try to maintain such a tradition, however uneasily. The separation of church from state in our country has made this difficult if not altogether impossible, however, and freedom of religious expression has created the possibility of separate religious groups for unconventional believers, along with groups that over the course of time must face the fact that many of their members or their young people no longer are moved as the first generation was.

Thus the differences between conventional and unconventional believers, differences that arise in any religious milieu, necessarily create in our society a perennial tension and pressure for new and more adequate religious forms. Because of their potential for dynamic growth, some such groups founded in the past have become in certain cases the conventional denominations of today, but in others these groups have persisted as groups of unconventional believers. Thus it is important to examine newly forming groups as an aid in the attempt to predict what religion in America will be like in future years.

Finally, we suggest that the rate of formation of new groups, the particular needs that they seem to fulfill, and the relation they bear to a society's older religious traditions are heavily conditioned by what is happening to the society as a whole. One important factor in America today is the widespread disillusionment with the values of an advanced technological society and with its religious traditions

6. For an examination of unusual contemporary religious groups with particular emphasis on expressions of the traditions of the East, see Robert S. Ellwood, Jr., *Religious and Spiritual Groups in Modern America* (Englewood Cliffs, N. J.: Prentice-Hall, Inc., 1973) and Jacob Needleman, *The New Religions* (Garden City, N. Y.: Doubleday and Company, Inc., 1970).

as well. In such a society group loyalties of all kinds are put under powerful stress. For many people, especially the educated young, the unconventional religious impulse leads to an impassioned inwardness, to interest in the contemplative religions of the East, and often to drug-induced mysticism. Since many individuals go in these directions because of high dissatisfaction with all the institutional forms they know, it is doubtful that for them the unconventional religious impulse will generate enduring groups. But this is by no means our whole story. The whole story is more rich and varied than most people realize; a source of part of the variety is groups that have roots in the ancient traditions that it has become fashionable to deride. The proof of opinions, after all, is in facts, and so we turn to a survey of how the quest for unconventional religious experience has been pursued across the broad spectrum of American religious groups.

Unconventional
Religious Groups

A TIME OF REBIRTH

One evening a pious and troubled man, seeking a religious assurance he had not yet experienced, went to a meeting at which the subject was "the change which God works in the heart through faith in Christ." Like many another person in the same spiritual predicament, this man had gone to the meeting unwillingly. He had tried hard to settle his religious questions and doubts, harder than all but a few in any age, but since he lived in a time when most people he knew thought that faith was a little silly, he was particularly unusual. But he did not give up easily in whatever he did, and this quest for faith seemed more important to him than anything else he could do, even than the academic career in which he had had good prospects by virtue of his intelligence, good training, and an appetite for hard work. What he most wanted, however, had so far eluded him, at least until this meeting; even afterward he was intelligent enough and skeptical enough to throw up a host of new questions. Yet the meeting was somehow decisive because, as he wrote later, "I felt my heart strangely warmed. I felt I did trust in Christ, Christ alone, for salvation; and an assurance was given me, that He had taken away my sins, even mine, and saved me from the law of sin and death." [1]

The language may not be exactly what you would find today, but it isn't really that different either. The important thing is that it follows an old pattern and in turn sets a pattern for any number of groups of unconventional believers down to the present time. The man was John Wesley, and the year of his conversion experience was 1738, when he was already in his early thirties. He was an Oxford graduate in a time when modern science had recently started taking its first giant steps following the work of the great Isaac Newton, a time when the typical university student felt that reason was a sounder guide to the truth of God than many of the tradi-

1. For Wesley's account of his conversion see *The Journal of John Wesley* (New York: Capricorn Books, 1963), p. 51.

25

tional church dogmas. When Wesley was in Oxford, his younger brother Charles, who was later to make a rich contribution to the hymnals still used in most Protestant churches, started a little group of interested students who called themselves the "Holy Club." In a way most unusual for that time, they discussed the Scriptures, prayed together, took communion regularly according to the forms of the Church of England, and in general ordered their lives so closely according to religious obligations that some sarcastic wits thought up the name that they later became proud of, "Methodists." John Wesley soon joined and became the dominant figure both in the group and in the religious movement that developed from it.[2]

Wesley and his helpers later scandalized conventional opinion, first by taking faith so seriously, then by taking it to other people, hosts of people who were being neglected by the conventional church—the workers in city industry and the poor of the slums that received the migrants from the increasingly depopulated countryside. The situation then resembles in many respects what is happening in America now. Wesley, responding to the need, was to make over city lofts into chapels, preach in the fields and on the streets, and gather his converts into small groups of people who supported each other by prayer, moral discipline, and mutual love. He inspired a group of powerfully dedicated preachers, many of whom came to America, lived down their English connections after the Revolutionary War, and soon built the Methodist Church into the largest Protestant denomination in the growing country. They did so by working tirelessly, as clergymen riding out on horseback to cover what were called "circuits" and bring the Gospel to the people, rather than waiting for the people to settle in towns and call them, as the New England preachers had thought was the right way to do things.

On the frontier early in the nineteenth century, Methodist preachers developed the institution of the "camp meeting," initiated by Presbyterians but actually much more in tune with the Methodists' own theology and traditions. These meetings were mass gatherings of people from a variety of religious backgrounds or from none at all. Preachers of many persuasions exhorted them to repent of their sins, at first in small groups but then in mass meetings in which the fervor of the most affected had the strongest possible influence on others. As the land became more settled, these meetings were regulated and toned down a bit in their emotional-

2. For the historical context of the rise of Methodism, see John Dillenberger and Claude Welch, *Protestant Christianity* (New York: Charles Scribner's Sons, 1954).

ism, and people in each locality were organized into congregations. Characteristic Methodist features remained, however—the stress on punishment of sin and the need for personal redemption, which could be confirmed in turn by a strict moral discipline directed to living a sober life. This was meant quite literally, for Methodists have always had a strong antipathy to alcohol and drinking, starting with the days when Wesley was appalled by what cheap gin was doing to the poor of London. But it also meant, by extension, the traditional truth that a good person would be known by the fruits of his life—honesty, uprightness, moderation, and charity toward those who had not yet seen the light.

Is this just history—that is, something that happened before the conditions of modern life were established, and that therefore has no importance for us? Anyone who thinks about history in a more than superficial way will find that it cannot be dismissed so easily, because history is the record of how living people responded to the pain and anxiety of their human existence. If you look carefully at how such responses are being made today, they do not look that different after all. At least much of what is happening today looks so much like what has happened to others in the past that some comparisons may help us understand our own times and give us some clues about what will happen in our own future.

Thus what Wesley started tells us a lot about unconventional believers—what they are looking for and what results from their searchings. His was the first religious movement that worked out its destiny in an essentially free religious situation, one in which government authorities and the church had little or no power to enforce conformity to an established system. Like other religious systems, it went to people with a purpose in mind, saying "This is what you need, this is what is good for you." But, unlike most others, it tried to make that judgment stand only by willing agreement. This emphasis on voluntary participation proved advantageous in the American colonies. The old Calvinist preachers of New England believed that people needed to be required to hear the preaching of a well-educated minister, no matter how they felt about it. Even the Presbyterians were hampered in the new situation by their belief that most people who heard them were destined to be damned. The Methodists felt that salvation was communicated by humbler people who knew what it felt like to be saved, and who knew how to speak in words that ordinary individuals understood. What they spoke about was the deeply felt message that the burden of sin was real, and terrible, but that it could be lifted from the shoulders of people who really repented and truly believed. For these preachers and people who accepted their message, only those would be damned who refused to hear and respond to the Gospel. Salvation was available if one only wanted it badly enough.

MODERN RELIGIOUS EXPERIENCE

This is why the story of Wesley's conversion appears at the start of this chapter. The story is a kind of model of modern religious experience, and it is valuable here for two basic reasons. First of all, it is a good illustration of what all of us take for granted, that religious truth is confirmed by a kind of emotional experience. What is that experience like? It is a unique feeling of finality, like Wesley's conversion experience and like that well described in the words of a Winnebago Indian who early in this century was converted from his tribal traditions under the power of the peyote cactus: " 'This is what it is,' I thought, 'this is what they all probably see and I am just beginning to find out.' " [3] The experience is basic, and it comes to you like an initiation into something new, no matter what your previous experience was. It takes you where you had not been before, and even though afterward you may find yourself slipping back to the old frame of mind, you know you do not have to stay there because you have been somewhere else. The imagery is almost inevitably geographic, but the point should be clear. A converted person is a different person in his own eyes.

It should also be clear that in this respect Wesley is the godfather of today's "Jesus people." He would be scandalized, of course, if he were brought to life today and were associated with any such idea as "getting high on Jesus." That phrase implies approval of intoxication, and it shows that many of us are considerably more tolerant than Wesley would have been of using chemicals to affect our minds. On the other hand, Wesley would understand very well the point that is made by this way of speaking. The Jesus freak may be a person who has given up drugs and now thinks of them as a means to escape the necessity of facing oneself. He thinks of himself as a person who was troubled, lost and once wandering but now converted, renewed, and redirected to the right path. In other words, faith for the Jesus freak is put to exactly the same test to which Wesley subjected it, the test of settling all fundamental doubts about oneself and the direction one's life is taking. The aptness of

3. Paul Radin, *The Autobiography of a Winnebago Indian* (New York: Dover Publications, Inc., 1963), p. 58.

this comparison across the centuries may be demonstrated by the fact that one of the most popular hymns of the Jesus movement, "Amazing Grace," was written by John Newton, a younger contemporary of John Wesley and like him a Church of England clergyman.

The second reason that the example of Wesley is important for our purposes is that by looking carefully at what happened to the Wesleyan movement, we can learn what to expect when people try to organize this bedrock religious experience into an ongoing social movement. Here the Indian's remark quoted above is instructive. He decided that the experience he was having was the same in essence as the experience of members of the group he was joining. He felt that what was happening to him had already happened to them. In other words, the motives for conversion lead people to seek an experience that not only transforms them but also binds them together in a group of people who "love one another," to use words once used about the small group of early Christians. People want to have unusual and profound experiences, but when they have them they want to understand them too, to know that the experiences mean something. This imperative operates especially in religion. In order to understand his own conversion, the believer interprets it in accordance with the ways in which he has learned to define and symbolize religious experience. This effort leads him to join a community whose members have seen the same vision. On the other hand, the uniqueness and power of conversion often generate a movement of religious change. The convert criticizes the institution he knew previously, since, as in Wesley's case and Luther's, the institution failed to comfort him until grace came from elsewhere. Or else no institution seems adequate to hold and reproduce the totality of what he has seen, and so he moves to change the old or build anew.

Thus the Methodist tradition begins very much as the work of an unconventional believer. Even though it has long since become a familiar and often a conventional presence in our religious life, the Methodist Church continues to give rise to innovating personalities, and it has done so all along. It is worth mentioning that the first important independent churches for black people in the United States were set up under Methodist auspices, early in the nineteenth century. And it may well be maintained that the Baptist churches, which enlisted so many blacks after the Civil War, were indirectly of Methodist origin. The Baptists had become Calvinists, for the most part, during the eighteenth century, and thus believed in predestination and the powerlessness of the individual to help himself in the quest for salvation. Later, however, they took up revival methods pioneered by Methodists and came to believe, like them, that people could choose to be reached by the grace of God.

It is interesting to see how many other people who were Methodists, or deeply affected by Methodist revivalism, became the founders of groups of unconventional believers in the years following John Wesley's time.[4] In some cases these new leaders were former Methodists who felt the need to start a movement responding more directly to their own needs and the needs of their time; their groups in turn have been the spiritual birthplaces of more recent groups. Even when there is no clear lineage from Wesley, it is still uncanny how often his experience and the church built upon it can be used to describe and explain the origins of other later movements and the courses they followed. It may be that the best test of whether a group remains spiritually satisfying to the unconventional believer is whether it continues to answer the religious problems he has tried to solve.

Our working definition of the churches of unconventional believers, therefore, is that they comprise groups of people characterized by the need to press religious questions further than ordinary people do, and that they tend to do so with an emotional intensity beyond what most people invest in religious participation. Such unconventional believers demand answers to questions of ultimate meaning, whereas other people live with a measure of doubt. Or they must have a warmth of feeling not attainable through conventional worship and, after their initial conversion, a means of assuring themselves that the change was real and permanent. They also require human associations that confirm this way of perceiving and responding to reality. People must love them for their faith, if you will; they in turn are ready to give much of themselves in gratitude for such assurances.

As we shall see later, such groups may be formed in traditional religious communities such as the Catholic Church or Judaism but certainly also in the midst of the established denominations of Protestantism. In part, however, the differences between

4. Joseph Smith, for example, was particularly impressed by the efforts of Methodists to win him to their church. Ellen White, cofounder of the Seventh-Day Adventist Church, was raised a Methodist. Charles Finney was a Congregationalist but adopted the Methodist doctrine of perfectionism. Holiness and Nazarene churches were offshoots of Methodism, and William Booth, founder of the Salvation Army, had been a Methodist clergyman. For several of these examples see Bryan Wilson, *Religious Sects* (New York: McGraw-Hill Book Company, 1970).

these various traditions are expressed in the differing forms taken by unconventional groups within them. At least until very recent times in America, traditional communities have either kept dissent "within the family" or have lost dissenters to the Protestant majority. The Protestant experience has been rather different, because since the establishment of religious freedom in America, and to some extent even before that, the unconventional religious tendency tended to be expressed through the creation of a new group, a new theology, a new denomination.

The reasons for this difference are many, but it may be a sufficient explanation that for Protestantism, unlike the more traditional faiths, the form of the church has never been taken for granted, but instead has always been in question. This was to some extent true even for the first New Englanders. They wanted to establish a truly religious community when they came to these shores, but they found themselves more willing to agree on the opinion that the Bible would reveal what such a community would be like than on what it actually should be like. In other words, community was an ideal for Protestants rather than a reality, and a new religious dynamic was likely to be expressed as a new form of the faith, a new church, rather than as a new tendency or group within the old church. At times, in fact, it seemed that acceptance of a new faith appealed to people as a means of testing their religious ingenuity.

A related point is that there was almost a kind of obligation among Protestants to go on creating new forms of their faith. This Protestant restlessness over the true form of the church, when combined with freedom to create new forms, produced a powerful tendency to reinforce those forms that worked, that gave people what they wanted in the form of religious experience, rather than told them what to believe and what to do. And since Protestants, like most people, were in most cases not unconventional believers, those who wanted a more intense experience found themselves facing settled interests, doubts, and compromises.

In the course of time this came to be true even within groups of what had been unconventional believers. Wesley foresaw that the habits he taught his people would most likely cause them to grow rich, and that on that account they could confidently be expected to lose their zeal for their faith.[5] But even that is not the whole story. It is, after all, not very easy to maintain oneself for a long

5. A classic statement by Wesley is quoted in Max Weber, *The Protestant Ethic and the Spirit of Capitalism* (New York: Charles Scribner's Sons, 1958), p. 175. See below, p. 163.

time in a community of love. Most people find it possible to settle for respectability in their religious group and to take their chances on love at home within their families. Thus for groups of unconventional believers to maintain themselves in their original state of religious dynamism requires a willingness to remain different, even to work at being so, for the sake of the particular characteristics the group maintains, and by virtue of the gains that members realize in not slipping into conventional patterns of behavior.

THE INTENTION OF UNCONVENTIONAL BELIEF

It should be emphasized that the distinction between conventional and unconventional believers, if it is to mean anything important, has to tell us something about the intentions behind what people do for the sake of their faith and as an expression of it. The dynamic quality in the faith of unconventional believers inevitably comes out in behavior that by the standards of ordinary people may be unusual, bizarre, or even repugnant.

With the passage of time several kinds of developments will change the significance of this behavior, and the meaning of the group may therefore change for those who belong to it. For one thing, other people may start behaving in a similar way, with the result that the original group no longer seems so unusual. The Methodists are a good example of this outcome. Alternatively, it may not seem appropriate to continue behaving in the original way. For example, the Quakers in the seventeenth century were noted for behavior that nowadays would be the mark of a Yippie or some similar group. That is, they dressed in sackcloth and ashes and disrupted what they considered unspiritual worship services; once a Quaker walked naked up the streets of an English town in an act of symbolic speech. From the nineteenth century to the present, however, the Quakers' response to the inner light that they believe is in all persons has been a much more decorous one.

Of course, the original generation passes on, and the group it composed will necessarily change unless a younger generation grows up willing to maintain the distinctiveness of the group. It is noteworthy that today the Old Order Amish, strict Mennonites, have won the right to continue educating their children in their own schools only through the eighth grade, and to refuse to send them on to public high schools of the rural communities where they live. The Amish descend from unconventional believers of the days of Martin Luther in the early sixteenth century, people who were too unconventional for Luther, and they realize that secular education encourages their young to take on the ways of the conventional world and thus be lost to them.

In other words, a group that wishes to maintain itself as a spiritual home for unconventional believers must keep alive a sense of its difference from the conventional world. Practices that once were distinctive lose their force unless they remain marks of an intention not to live as other people live or think as they think. They become only the things habitually done by everybody who belongs to the group, but the inner tension is missing. The Protestant past is rich with the proliferation of groups that were begotten out of some highly personal religious vision that later drifted out of focus. Is it so different to put on the uniform of the Salvation Army or to join the "Billy Graham team," when to do so involves joining a group as organized as many modern corporations? You cannot easily answer this question simply by jotting down the details of the ways in which such groups look different from other people. The differences may be habits and not the marks of groups of truly unconventional believers.

What is different about Protestantism, as we have said, is that in so many such cases a particular organization has grown up to perpetuate a particular vision. It is not that unconventional opportunities do not arise within the established denominations, for, as we shall see, they do in perhaps the same variety and availability as in the traditional churches. But the point is that we live as heirs of an extraordinary time, in a curious land in which a host of unconventional religious impulses staked out independent claims or elbowed others aside in the appeal to religious allegiance. Many of these groups still exist, and we find ourselves interested in whether they still maintain their old character and give scope for the genuinely unconventional. Others are still coming into being, and we want to assess their prospects of staying with us and offering something to people in years to come that they cannot find in their present church or synagogue. We want to see what some of these groups are like and also have some means of evaluating them.

On the other hand, it is not really possible in a single book to cover the entire field. One could write a statistical catalogue, which would give but little nourishment and no flavor. Or one could choose a few groups for their intrinsic interest and describe them, making no attempt to place them in any meaningful relation to each other. Any choice of groups is largely arbitrary, of course, since a single individual's perspective and resources are limited. Thus the weaknesses of this book lie more in the second direction than the first. But it tries to reduce the difficulty by the selection of groups that illustrate the whole range of interests that have been expressed perennially in unconventional religious efforts.

Two large classes of groups that might have been included have not been, because in both cases they have been treated well by other authors in recent works. These are, first, groups that derive from Eastern religions. For the first time Americans have been given, for example, the possibility of achieving spiritual enlightenment with authentic Zen masters in monastic seclusion while others have been induced openly to participate in such distinctly unconventional activities as chanting the praises of the Hindu god Krishna in Times Square in New York City. Secondly, we exclude many of the effects of the enthusiasm for Jesus that has surfaced largely among young people and made them into "Jesus People," in some cases leading them out of the wilderness of drug abuse and in many others providing a kind of natural transition for the electric feelings aroused by rock-music records, concerts, and festivals. Others have described this new enthusiasm for Jesus, but in any case it is questionable how long this enthusiasm will last. Where such enthusiasm has provided the motive for communal living, the results are more relevant; in the final chapter we shall treat this subject briefly and suggest how an interest in it may be pursued further.

What follows in this section of the book, therefore, is a set of descriptions of groups, some of which have continuity with the past but all of which have continued vitality in the present. The motive for writing about several of these groups is that not much responsible work has been done on them. Another motive, as has been indicated already, stems from the feeling that many unconventional possibilities are being ignored among familiar institutions because they are mistakenly identified as stagnant old establishments. But perhaps another motive is the most important of all. In our time many religious groups compete furiously with each other in claiming to have the truth. It is a temptation to dismiss them all as having no claim on our attention just because they claim too much. But to do so would be a mistake, because all these groups have much to tell us about what it means to people when they can take their faith seriously.

The Evangelist
and the Decision
for Christ

A remarkable documentary movie that opened to audiences in 1972
pictured part of the career of a young man named "Marjoe," who
was trained by his parents to be a dynamic evangelist. At the age of
four he was ordained a clergyman in order to be able to perform
weddings. He learned by heart the words and gestures, and he developed what can only be called the "stage presence" necessary to his
work. Little Marjoe took to the work so well that he became a spell-
binder and induced people to make offerings of large sums of money
that he subsequently accuses his father of pocketing. Significantly,
though, Marjoe himself does not come through as a cynical exploiter
in the film. To be sure, he knows that many of his best effects are
calculated, that they produce a religious response from his crowd
without any corresponding commitment from him. Yet he also
recognizes that what he does serves his own needs as well. He likes
to do his act. He likes the response he gets from people. He remarks
that he would probably have become a rock musician if he had not
been an evangelist. From his standpoint, the psychological rewards
are the same.[1]

1. The film "Marjoe," widely shown in 1972, was something of an exposé of
revivalism by an "insider," Marjoe Gortner. Popular magazines carried a number
of interviews with him.

A number of inferences can be drawn from this example. Most importantly, it shows that popular religion and popular entertainment draw on many of the same emotional responses both from the audience and from the performers. The ultimate purposes of the respective efforts may be very different, as they undoubtedly are when you compare a rock musician hungry for enormous sums of money with a sincere evangelist interested in how many souls he has won for Christ. But there have been cynical evangelists, as well as popular musicians more interested in their art than in earning money. Thus you have to look hard at the similarities and conclude that in the interplay between the dynamic figure on stage and the many people watching and listening, many of the same emotional processes and responses are involved.

Thus it may become easier to understand how a rock music enthusiast will be able to change from devotion to the Beatles, the Rolling Stones, or whatever other group is at the top at the moment, to devotion to Christ. True, a considerable alteration of behavior and outlook is required, including the adoption of specific beliefs and moral patterns of conduct, and the rejection of the anti-establishment pleasure-seeking that characterizes so many members of the so-called "youth culture." But doubtless such changes are foreshadowed, in those who make them, by guilt and remorse, perhaps a lingering loyalty to what parents have tried to encourage, and the desire to fall back on accepted values. Instead of the "devilish" singer who inspires an almost frantic response but does not come through as personally interested in his followers, the evangelist presents himself with equal feeling, with music and a strong appeal to the heart, but also with an appeal to a new life, a better life, and often with a personal promise of great sincerity.

In the electronic age both popular music and popular evangelism have amplified their power with microphones and huge loudspeakers. Of the two music, naturally, has gone much farther in the search for special sound effects, but it is remarkable to what degree the "old-time religion" is communicated by electronic means—not only made more audible at a mass meeting but also broadcast on radio and television, as well as printed, mailed, and in general sent abroad by every method used by commercial interests to get a message across.

Many careers in modern evangelism have been founded on the use of thoroughly up-to-date methods like these. The basic style was set almost a century and a half ago by a man named Charles Grandison Finney, a lawyer by training, who experienced a divine call to preach and later developed self-conscious techniques of evangelism that he called "new measures." Finney used these new measures systematically to win more souls for Christ. Though at first he was a Presbyterian, Finney, like Wesley and many others, rejected the teaching of predestination because he thought people were able to accept some of the responsibility for their own salvation. He trained others to follow him, and each succeeding generation has produced similar evangelists of note. The names of Dwight L. Moody and his song leader Sankey are still familiar to many, as is that of the flamboyant Billy Sunday.[2]

What is important is that this form of unconventional religion has not declined. Those who think of it only as something reminiscent of former times forget not only Marjoe and many other evangelists with local reputations, particularly in the heavily Protestant South—they also forget a man like the faith healer Oral Roberts, whose evangelism has been so successful that he has founded and developed a university named after him and devoted to Christian principles. Certainly the extraordinary amounts of energy poured into such efforts qualifies them as unconventional religion.

Let us look at one example in more detail. The scene is a new baseball stadium in a major city while the home team is away. One essential of the evangelist's art is the ability to gather a large audience. Since even cathedrals are too small for such audiences and theaters are inadequate, modern cities offer only the arenas for sporting events as suitable gathering-places for such crowds. As a matter of fact the stadium lends an air of informality quite appropriate to the revival style. True, the people attending are better dressed than they would be for a sporting event. They expect to be moved, but in a reverential, not a boisterous way. Furthermore, most of them are already churchgoers. Like Wesley, they have been constant in their pursuit of their faith and worthiness in the sight of God. Perhaps to underscore the contrast with sporting events, there is no admission charge. People stream in from the nearby rapid-transit station, individually or in family or larger groups. Numbers of yellow school buses in the adjacent parking lot have brought in groups of churchgoers from suburban areas. As they enter, they find the sections of seats beside home plate already filled

---

2. On revivalism in general, see William G. McLoughlin, Jr., *Modern Revivalism* (New York: The Ronald Press Company, 1959). McLoughlin has also published a critical biography of Billy Graham. There is an authorized biography by John Pollock (New York: McGraw-Hill Book Company, 1966). Generally negative evaluations of Graham's work can be found in back issues of such liberal Protestant journals as *The Christian Century* and *Christianity and Crisis,* generally positive ones in the more conservative *Christianity Today.*

with people much like themselves, except that these have volunteered to sing as members of the great choir that lines out the hymns. The stadium does not fill completely, but a substantial crowd fills the sections of seats along the baselines in both the upper and the lower decks.

Facing the crowd from where second base would be on a playing day is a sizable raised platform with a number of chairs and a central lectern with microphone connected to a powerful public address system. Off toward third base is a separate stand for the keyboard of a large electric organ. From a podium closer to the stands the song leader conducts the choir and the organist in familiar evangelical hymns. In recent years television cameras have also been utilized to carry the proceedings to a wider audience. At such moments the cameras pan out over the thousands of singers, while the sound channels carry the words of the traditional message.

There is nothing surprising about the conduct of the meeting itself, and certainly there is no hysteria, but rather an unmistakable air of sincerity, authority, and basic good humor that carries through even on rainy nights when the crowd is diminished and the usual effectiveness is dampened. After the crowd is settled and has heard or joined in some of the singing, the platform fills and the meeting officially begins. One of the associate evangelists leads in prayer and then introduces other people who have been sitting with him. A famous singer now in the twilight of her career rises to give a musical testimony to the power of faith in her life. Other witnesses speak of what Christ has done for them. There is a young man of Puerto Rican lineage, who tells how he was converted from a life of petty crime and gang violence and how he is now preaching among those who need the same message he once heard. Others stand and are identified as local clergymen noted for their evangelical efforts or as well-known individuals who have turned to Christ and found their lives transformed. As the last preliminary to the introduction of the featured evangelist himself, the singer rises who for years has been identified with the evangelist and has done much to inspire listeners to the evangelist's message.

BILLY GRAHAM

Thus far our description has been unspecific because the methods used at such meetings by various evangelists are very much the same. But despite many similarities of technique, the evangelists are unique individuals, inspire very personal followings, and deserve individual attention themselves. The foregoing description was of one evening of Billy Graham's crusade in New York's Shea Stadium in the summer of 1970. On the one hand, it would be much the same for the crusade held in Anaheim, Calif., the previous autumn, but on the other hand, few other evangelists, if any, are in the same league. (The baseball comparison is not inappropriate, considering the fact that the young Graham had a great drive to excel as a baseball player.) Few other speakers could continue to draw such crowds in city after city, especially considering the continuous exposure Graham has had on radio and television, to say nothing of his presence at the White House during Richard Nixon's presidency. Billy Graham is without doubt the premier evangelist of our time, and it is worth deep consideration that he has made a mark on the lives of many more people than any of the famous evangelists of former times.[3]

The singer of the Billy Graham team is George Beverly Shea. Shea was already well known on Chicago radio when Graham, as a dynamic local preacher newly graduated from Wheaton College in Illinois, approached him for assistance in mounting an effective radio program in 1944. At this time Graham began working on evangelical rallies using the banner "Youth for Christ" under the auspices of conservative Baptist clergymen and businessmen. In successive years just after World War II, Graham went on evangelizing trips to England. The first was not very successful; on the second trip, Graham was accompanied by a new song leader named Cliff Barrows, and things went a little better. Shea and Barrows have been prominently associated with Graham down to the present time. After just a few years of experience together, they acquired the necessary professionalism to carry the stress of ever larger meetings. Their organization began its work in 1949. In that year a three-week campaign held in a large tent in Los Angeles reached a turning point when several people well known to the public were converted. The ailing publishing tycoon William Randolph Hearst took an interest in Graham's activities through a maid who was caring for him, and he gave Graham nationwide publicity in his newspapers. The campaign was extended to eight weeks, filling the enlarged tent with more than 9,000 people. Fourteen years later, in 1963, the crusade in Los Angeles was able to fill the enormous Coliseum with many more than 100,000 people. Obviously, what moves

3. Newspaper accounts of a meeting in Seoul, Korea, early in June, 1973, spoke of a crowd of half a million people, the largest by far of Graham's career.

so many people over so long a period of time has to be taken seriously.

The essence of the force of the Billy Graham Evangelistic Association must be looked for in the person after whom it was named in 1950. His group of workers is a team, and a large and effective organization has grown up around him, but none of this organization would mean much if Graham were not there as a central stimulus. At all his meetings, no matter how modestly he conducts himself in relation to his coworkers, Billy Graham's praying and preaching are the event to which everything else is preliminary. At the Shea Stadium meeting described above, when he was introduced the stirring of the crowd ceased and a sense of rising expectation was apparent. All eyes were fixed on his tall figure, the bright color of his well-fitted jacket emphasized by the strong lighting focused on him. Graham is a handsome man with wavy blond hair and the look of authority. He carries himself well, so that his physical presence inspires confidence. His surroundings when he preaches enforce the impression he makes—the crowds, the sense of something out of the ordinary, the lights and the music, the amplification of the voice—but the look and the voice ring true. Anyone listening to him has no doubt that Graham means what he says; that a man so well endowed in personal qualities means what he is saying makes a difference to his audience.

Billy Graham asks the audience to pray with him, not in a formal way but with a personal "I" and a personal "you." The prayer is focused on the significance of this particular evening, this meeting, and on the personal needs of those who are present. The spirit of God is invoked in the classical evangelistic way to bless the gathering, to come into the hearts of those who are distressed, and to change them. After the prayer Graham greets his listeners, thanks them for coming, and urges them to return every night for the rest of the series of meetings. This is a minimal step that requires no further effort than a subway ride, but it is important for the effect it may have on others. Large meetings day after day are a witness to what Christians call "the world" in terms that it has to take seriously. The intention, of course, is to involve as many people as possible. Some critics of Graham's work are uncomfortable with his stress on numbers, but it is noteworthy that those who respond to the man feel touched personally by him, and it is probable that Graham and his representatives provide more individual attention than many people receive from their own ministers, and on a deeper level.

The sermon is simple and effective in theme and outline.

Graham's North Carolina accent has been somewhat modified by the breadth of his experience, but it is a good vernacular for popular communication. He has long been known for the final sentence of his radio broadcasts, "May the Lord bless you real good," which for many is all the more welcome just because it is ungrammatical. What comes through especially is a feeling of conviction and sincerity, the sense that this man can be believed. His sermon begins with either a biblical text that can be given an extended moral significance or a discussion of a contemporary problem. Alternatively, Graham will begin with a story or anecdote: "Yesterday a young man called me on the telephone and asked what he could do about a problem he had." Such a beginning leaves an opening for several lines of development: the preacher can comment on how common the predicament is and what it indicates about the present state of things; he can compare it to a similar situation in the Bible; or he can examine the case in more detail and show how the traditional religious answer is not only right but practical as well. These are not mutually exclusive approaches, a number of them being capable of reinforcing each other.

No part of Graham's approach is especially novel. Much of the power of such preaching lies in the years of experience that make it possible to seem to be speaking extemporaneously. Of course, this freedom to depart from a prepared text is the product of years of work delivering the evangelistic message to live audiences—in early days, to anyone who would listen. It is also a product of simplification—reduce the content of what you are going to say to a few basic points, and in any given sermon arrange your scriptural text and illustrative material around two or three basic ideas. Critics have accused Graham, as they have all famous evangelists, of unduly simplifying the Gospel. The charge is partly true, but it is a lot less true when you examine the overall content of such a man's preaching, which will cover a surprising amount of ground. What is significant is that the evangelist tends to concentrate solely on the need for personal redemption, the assertion that Jesus Christ is a resource adequate for all such needs and the proof of such assertions in quotations from the Bible. People who think deeply about religious ideas argue that the full truth of Christianity cannot be communicated so simply. To be sure, most evangelists would freely acknowledge the force of that argument. Their defense is that subtlety is not appropriate to the situation and indeed distorts the message by confusing people. On the evidence of American religious history, their success in drawing people to the faith is a powerful argument.

When Billy Graham speaks, it is hard to remain indifferent, and it is also hard to be actively hostile to him, since he is so modest in what he says on his own behalf. It is not his message, he declares, but God's message, delivered through the life and teachings of Jesus— his voice always rises on the first syllable of Jesus—and unmistakably guaranteed by the promise of salvation in the Bible. The word "Bible" is treated in the same way, with the accent on the first syllable of the word giving the implication that the Bible and Christ are really one. A typical picture of Graham preaching, especially in his younger days when he was closer to a fundamentalist position than he is now, would show him holding the Bible open to his text in his left hand, his right hand raised with forefinger pointed upward in a gesture of admonition. One of his most effective devices, according to accounts of his earlier campaigns, was to single out individuals, not by name but in terms of a moral problem, by saying something like, "I have a feeling that someone here tonight wants to accept Jesus but won't let himself give up his sins." Some felt that the finger pointed at them, and left in anger, only to return later and make what Graham calls a "decision for Christ." Many, of course, have come to the meeting ready to hear such a message and to interpret it as intended for them. Graham's way of speaking seems well-nigh perfectly attuned to their needs. The essence of all mass meetings is that the people present are related primarily to the leader rather than to each other, and that the presence of others, rather than being experienced as competition for the leader's attention, somehow magnifies the effect of his preaching and quiets doubts that might lead to a refusal to hear and respond to his message.

THE DECISION

The climax of the service is the call for decisions, what used to be termed the "altar call" in Baptist churches. This procedure has been adapted to large stadiums for mass meetings; it is also part of people's expectations when they know how the evangelist works. Thus the sermon is a "converting ordinance," to use an old theological term. It is not just to be listened to, but it encourages a response. The lordship of Christ, the direct rule of God in your life, living in holiness, and the like, all are terms for the new existence held out to you not just as an opportunity but as your obligation. This is because you have the power to decide for Christ, according to the evangelical idea of Christianity, and if you fail to do so, you are stubborn, resistant to the change that may not make you richer but will straighten out your relations both with God and with the people in your life. An unscrupulous preacher could use such techniques to frighten people into conversion. Listening to Graham, you do feel considerable pressure to get to your feet and join the crowd walking up to the rostrum, especially if you have come to the meeting with family or friends who decide to go forward. In fairness, though, it cannot be said that Graham abuses his influence. It could be argued that some pressure is needed in order to get people over the psychological hurdle in the way of doing something they want to do but find hard to do. Certainly it is an impressive sight, as the preacher stands with head bowed, to see hundreds of people walking forward from all parts of the crowd to stand before the speaker's platform. At Shea Stadium, where the New York Mets baseball team had become world-beaters just the year before, several could not resist the chance to take a brief detour to sit for a moment on the bench in the home team's dugout. It was as if they could join with champions in two ways at once.

What have you decided when you make a decision for Christ and go forward to the speaker's rostrum? You have made an unconventional response, for despite the number of people who decide, the number who simply leave after the meeting is far greater. Presumably you want to go beyond the usual religious life you've been used to, and it would be a disservice to you if nothing were changed but your own mind. In some ways what happens after the decision is the most impressive part of the team effort, for after Billy Graham has stimulated people to make a new, or a renewed, commitment, a well-organized administrative system goes into operation to translate decisions into effective church membership. Long ago—in fact in the days of John Wesley's work—preachers of religious revivals were often all too ready to let people conclude that their own familiar clergymen were "dead" men, meaning by that that they were dry speakers, untouched by the fire of the true Christian. Thus preachers who "itinerated," or traveled about, were apt to be criticized for stirring up divisions, for being "censorious." [4] In fact such activity did break off groups of the unconventional believers of that day, with the resulting birth of countless new religious groups. For the Methodists, itinerancy became a standard technique for winning souls to Christ as the western wilderness was settled. But after the end of frontier days there was a tendency for evangelists to work

4. Volume I of *American Christianity*, edited by H. Shelton Smith, Robert T. Handy, and Lefferts A. Loetscher (New York: Charles Scribner's Sons, 1960), has several primary-source accounts, including one entitled by the editors "The Harvard Faculty Rebukes Whitefield," p. 330.

out at least truces with the denominational clergymen of the settled towns. Graham long ago decided to cooperate as much as possible with local churches and clergy, even with obviously reluctant ones, for the sake of avoiding such criticism, and, more positively, for the sake of confirming the decisions of those touched by his message.

So when you have made your decision, and then made your way forward with others, you are assigned to a counselor who if possible is your age and is as educated as you. The few members of the professional staff of the traveling team are supplemented by large numbers of volunteers from the more willing churches of the vicinity, people themselves of an evangelical faith and a high degree of dedication. They are trained in advance to talk with you, to pray with you, and to refer you to an appropriate church in your town in the unlikely event that you are not already a church member. They record information about you that is relayed to another group of volunteers. In Shea Stadium the press facilities were full, with some volunteers answering telephones but most working to classify and direct the cards of those who had come forward. Names are recorded on the lists of the Billy Graham Evangelical Association in Minneapolis, Minnesota, and the information is also referred to the clergymen of churches near where the people live or to which they belong as members.

In the weeks that follow, at least according to plan, the decision for Christ is supported by efforts in several directions. The counselors are encouraged to keep in touch with every person they spoke to, and many of them do. From the Minneapolis headquarters come questions in Bible study. You read passages of the Bible and answer questions on them. When you return the answers they are corrected and new questions are issued. If the clergyman of your church is sympathetic to Graham's work, he too may act on the information he receives from the organization. Ideally, a crusade will stimulate growth in church membership and, more to the point, bring into churches people heartily committed to serve the Lord. All too often new church members are half-hearted, members largely for social reasons. Those who come from a Billy Graham crusade are full of religious energy and ready to work.

QUESTIONS AND NEEDS

But at this point a host of questions arises. Do those who make decisions for Christ expect too much of the churches they go back to? Can any church sustain such energies? Does the decision stand in memory as a kind of "peak experience," to which nothing else measures up, or is something of permanent value gained from it? For our purposes, in what ways does the experience of Billy Graham answer the needs of the unconventional believer? In reply, one must say that what goes on in most churches is unexciting and conventional most of the time. It is probably unreasonable to expect things to be much different, for clergymen have much to do besides preach, and many of them neither wish to work the way Graham does nor would find it possible to do so. For them the church is an everyday matter in which changes are often small and happen in their own time rather than by evangelistic techniques, however sincerely employed. Thus a real difficulty arises when their parishioners are moved by evangelical preaching like Graham's. He makes everyday realities come into question. It seems possible to change them, and you are convinced that he has laid on you the burden of finding ways to feel continually renewed by the Christian experience.

Wesley's answer to this problem was his doctrine of Christian perfection. After being converted you could hope to come near to perfect righteousness in the sight of God. The revivalists who followed Wesley have similarly looked for ways to help people feel that the conversion experience has really worked a permanent change in them. The typical Protestant version of perfection has been to make the avoidance of personal sins into a moral code and to define as sins such indulgences as drinking, smoking, and popular entertainment that encourages sensuality and especially illicit sexuality.

It is not really pertinent to criticize as naïveté the evangelist's concentration on such themes, for those themes are often the central personal preoccupations of even the most sophisticated people. Instead, the real issue posed by the revivalist impulse is whether it is right to demand that religious achievement be measured by how changed one feels and how well armed one has become against old temptations. The evangelist encourages you to expect your new self to be sustained after the conversion experience by what is called "assurance of salvation," and by a personal sense of relationship with Jesus on the same emotional basis as your conversion. How possible is it to receive the same experience again and again?

It might be argued, on the contrary, that when you change your ways after being affected by a powerful emotional or religious experience, you can't expect the same kind of feeling to be repeated when you need help in sticking to the new ways. Recall the case of the young woman who felt regenerated by the experience of using drugs. Afterwards she decided against repeating the experience and found that a new ability was needed, the need to treat her body with respect and the disciplined maturity to sustain this commitment whether she felt like it or not. With regard to evangelism, it may be that learning how to make a decision for Christ may teach you nothing about how to live the rest of your life as a Christian and may even make that more difficult.

Similarly, many discussions of the value of Billy Graham's work center on the issue of whether or not his converts remain active church members and therefore justify the great effort and expense committed to bringing them in. Much of this discussion has a partisan ring to it, because the friendly voices want to prove his value and enemies to discount it. Yet often both sides seem to miss the point, because they both accept without much question a numerical standard of evaluation. So many persevering church members against so many backsliders is the issue of these discussions, but few ask if this numerical issue is really what is at stake. Surely there are many seemingly good causes in which equal or greater amounts of effort and money have been expended in futile ways, but that does not make the causes bad ones. In any case, the testimony of all those who consider their encounters with Billy Graham as deeply meaningful in their lives is not an indication of futility. Nor is it a particularly strong argument to show that the people he reaches are generally not new converts in the sense of being strangers to the church. As we have said previously, the majority of those who make decisions for Christ at Graham's meetings are already church members or associated with a church in some way. This, of course, is true of the vast majority of people in America; thus it would be unfair to expect a large number of the converts to be new in an absolute sense. In other words, Graham's value is not to be decided on the basis of an effect on the growth of church membership. The real question is what value the experience of relating to him holds for those who do so, whether the unconventional response he generates is a good or a bad thing.

There are two possible ways for the experience to bear fruit in people's lives. Either it becomes the motivation for radically changing their behavior and for joining and continuing in a church to help confirm the change, or it remains a memorable experience valuable in itself, perhaps as a stage in growing up but not necessarily as the start of a total transformation. In the first case, the problem is that the Graham team comes to a city only once, or returns to larger cities only after a period of several years. The follow-up organization, the radio program and *Decision* magazine, the occasional televising of a crusade in another city, and the mailings from Minneapolis, while admirable as reminders and even as a kind of "media church," simply do not recreate the original experience. Anyone who requires that must be disappointed. The churches to which people are referred, on the other hand, are bound to be of uncertain quality as places of spiritual nurture for Graham's converts. Surveys of his results show that churches that gain the most members after his visit are those whose point of view is closest to his, as might be expected. Other congregations are unchanged and may even be negatively affected if some of their members have come to expect something like Graham's power.

What if we say, however, that the decision for Christ, while it may be a sufficiently powerful experience to transform some lives and generate lifelong devotion to Christian causes in the church, should really be evaluated on a different basis? It may be that the decision for Christ is less important for its permanent effect on the churches than for its nature as a spontaneous response to a particular personal need. It is certainly significant, for example, that a disproportionate number of people who come forward at Graham's meetings are adolescents. It is significant that he began his work under the banner of Youth for Christ. In fact, the adolescent years have always been the classic age for religious conversion. Psychologists typically explain this in terms of the strains caused by physical maturation and the social needs and obligations connected with this change, together with the great difficulties people have establishing their own identity in societies like ours. At such a time a strong religious commitment may help to set some boundaries and reduce uncertainty in life. Of course it may also be a mistake if it only offers an escape from problems that sooner or later must be solved. But it may be that for some people a temporary escape is useful and even necessary as a preparation for solving an emotional problem. It may not matter if an adolescent's decision for Christ becomes a lifetime commitment, so long as it is helpful for a time.

More positively, adolescence is the time when religious questions are raised most urgently and can be taken more seriously than at any other times of life. It is a rare adult who does not feel that his mature responsibilities have enforced compromises in the fine moral vision he had as a youth. Often this feeling brings with it a sense of disillusionment and cynicism about all moral commitments, especially if the youthful vision was never translated into action. Perhaps better off is the adult who in adolescent years made a commitment, tried to live up to it, and in the process learned something realistic about his own and other peoples' moral capabilities. In the older days of revivalism, more was made of the fear of hell and the promise of paradise than is generally credible nowadays. Thus the decision for Christ is more clearly an answer to a here-and-now need, but it is also the clearest image many people ever get of what it might mean to live by faith alone. In difficult times this vision may again and again reappear and sustain them.

To the extent that this is the case for people moved by Billy Graham's appeal, how important is it that they become and remain active church members? Graham's organization would not be happy to think that the response he generates in people spoils them for many local churches, but that may be the truth of the matter. Thus the old evangelical tension between the itineraters and the settled clergy may still persist, despite the best of intentions on the part of Billy Graham and his staff. In the last decade or so he has shown himself much concerned with the opinions of local clergy, not just because that is important for the success of his crusades, but also because he cares about Christian community and wants to be regarded as a builder of that community, not a destroyer.

Nevertheless, the problem for the churches may always remain. After all, the essence of what you meet in encountering Billy Graham is the sense of an intensely personal relation established between the two of you, just as it must have been when the Christian community was first founded. As we have indicated, it is impossible to maintain such a relation with so many people, despite the genuine effort to do so. Yet even though the attempt does not succeed, need it be judged a failure? You may say so only in the face of the witness of those many individuals for whom the event has been truly decisive, even if only for a brief period of their lives. Many an unconventional believer feels he owes his spiritual life to Billy Graham or to one of the many other colorful and powerful figures who make the faith an intensely personal message.

Saints of the Latter Day

The unconventional believer feels his faith deeply, but does it follow that such feeling demands the stimulus of an extraordinary emotional experience or the drama of a decision for Christ? Not at all. One of the most dynamic groups of unconventional believers draws its strength from a deep moral commitment to the everyday tasks of family living. It is the Church of Jesus Christ of Latter-day Saints, more commonly known as the Mormon Church, a group that has been identified historically with several regions of the country—not only the state of Utah, where the group now is predominant, but other places as well.

Initially, therefore, it may be illuminating to examine this group in the light of the regional differences that must be considered in any serious treatment of the religious life of America. Each part of the country has its particular regional traditions, sometimes developed into tourist attractions but often little known outside the vicinity. Some regional landmarks are geographical features like hot springs or oddly shaped mountain crags, and some have ethnic or historical significance, for example the abandoned pueblos or the Gettysburg battlefield. One landmark with a strictly religious meaning is called the Hill Cumorah. It is located in western New York State between two small towns named Palmyra and Manchester, a bit north of the New York Thruway, somewhat nearer Rochester than Syracuse but too far from either to be caught up in the process of urban development. Each year in late July large numbers of people are drawn to a pageant staged on the western side of the hill.

Except for this event, Palmyra would be difficult to distinguish from many towns built during the days of the Erie Canal and now no longer prosperous. Yet it saw the beginning of what may well be the most important of the unconventional religious groups of America, the Mormons.

The Hill Cumorah is not naturally a noteworthy location. It is not a very high hill nor even so separate from others as to be prominent. It is more than walking distance from the town, and few people live along the country road that runs north from the thruway to Palmyra. But the hillside has been converted into an outdoor theater for the pageant, which is repeated each evening for a week. Across the road two large fields have been cleared for a parking area for thousands of cars, and toward the end of the week the fields are full long before dusk. Many kinds of vehicles are in evidence, from compacts to oversized campers. What is most interesting about them is the variety of license plates. There are many more cars from the Far West than would be expected even in a national park. Most conspicuous, of course, are the many vehicles from Utah, the citadel of the Mormon faith. For these people, accustomed to journeying abroad for the sake of their religion, the trip to the Hill Cumorah has the quality of a pilgrimage, and on reflection you realize that an important element of the uniqueness of the place is the fact that America has few shrines. Spanish and French Roman Catholic settlement has left a few, such as the shrine of Ste. Anne de Beaupré in the Canadian province of Quebec, but the Puritan hostility to saints and shrines has left the would-be field of holy places pretty much to builders of monuments to national or local history.

Thus in a curious way the Mormon faith, as a late product of a distinctly visionary and unconventional strain of Protestant thinking, has tended to follow older patterns of religious behavior, although, of course, adding in the process a number of innovations of its own. It does so, however, under its claim of being a faith of the New World, not of the Old. When the early Puritan settlers of Massachusetts came to establish what Governor John Winthrop called a "cittee upon a hill," they did so with Europe in mind, with the idea that what they did would be a good example to the "old country." Their successors were somewhat bewildered by the needs of the country that came into being here, bound as they were to the attempt to perfect what they had known in England. One of the first groups to give up dependence on English models was the Mormon faith, which is therefore much more an American creation out of an American heritage than was the faith of the Puritans. To be sure, the Mormon faith was not created out of entirely new materials, for it is a variant of Christianity—but it grew in the wake of several stages of revival fervor, in consciousness of the needs of frontier and rural areas, and particularly out of a sense that America had come to represent the old world in opposition to which another New World had to be created.

Thus the Hill Cumorah pageant presents a faith history on a grand scale, based on events, peoples, and places nowhere to be found in standard histories of the ancient world. A section of the hillside has been cleared of trees, and the woods remaining on either side serve as the wings of a great outdoor stage. At various levels are platforms and rostra on which the many scenes are played, and concealed in the nearby trees and shrubs is a magnificent sound system. At the top of the hill, carefully tended shrubbery spells out the name "Cumorah" in letters large enough to be read from a low-flying airplane. Floodlights and spotlights are directed at significant points, and at the top of a spectator's field of vision is a flag-pole from which flies a great American flag. As the daylight fades, the details of the hillside merge into a dark backdrop from which they will be singled out by fingers of light. In the dusk, familiar hymns begin to sound from the hidden loudspeakers, sung in strong voice by the celebrated Mormon Tabernacle Choir in recordings made in Salt Lake City. Thus far, apart from the rather inaccessible setting, nothing is very unusual.

The crowd still gathers; many have brought folding chairs. In the center of the audience the seats are formed by painted boards held up by cinder blocks. The moon rises on one side of the sky, and the lights of a passing jetliner glide into the distance. Suddenly, at the top of the hill costumed figures appear in a flood of white light, young men representing angels and holding up long golden trumpets while brass fanfares blare from the speakers. Then the episodes of the story follow one after the other in a huge costume drama that is America's closest approach to Oberammergau's enactment of the Passion story.

The elements of this story are far less familiar, however. They tell a history of men who long ago attempted to obey God's law of righteousness but were finally defeated. A young man in shirt sleeves, Joseph Smith, is shown the place where on this very hillside hundreds of years ago the prophet Moroni, righteous son of a noble but dying people, buried golden plates, inscribed in "reformed Egyptian" with the sacred history of his people. It is Moroni, returned as a "resurrected personage," who leads Smith to the particular spot on the hillside and empowers him to read the ancient writings. The pageant flashes back over the text, sometimes with narrators reading the curious story in language like that of the old King James Version of the Bible. But the story is strange, for it concerns itself only intermittently with the people of Israel and the early Christians. Prophets defend the ways of God before kings, but the names of the supposedly historical figures are not to be found in the Bible. Valiant warriors vow to obey the will of God, and the remnant of a holy nation goes not into exile at Babylon but onto shipboard, sailing unnumbered miles to a foreign shore, there to fight for righteousness among people who even practice the ultimate degradation, human sacrifice. The story touches familiar ground only in its relating of the fate of God's own son, who comes among men only to be put to death by crucifixion high on the hill.

MORMON ORIGINS

Where did such a story come from, and how is it that its portrayal on a rural hillside can draw thousands of people on a summer evening at the cost of considerable effort? It is a colorful spectacle, well produced, and certainly an unusual event. But it is also the holy history of the Mormons, a transcription of some of the more critical episodes of the Book of Mormon, which for Mormons has a scriptural authority equivalent to that of the Bible. Because of this claim, both the contents of the book and the story of how it came to be given to the saints of these latter days are part of the message that Mormons feel obligated to communicate to others. The other part of that message, perhaps the more important part, consists of the community that was founded on the basis of this new revelation, a community more unified than any other group of similar size, a community with a history of persecution probably more severe than that endured by any other religious group in American history, apart from the pagan Indians who lived here when the settlers came. The migrations of the group to a barren wilderness took place little more than a century ago and are themselves a story worth retelling, though they form no part of the Hill Cumorah pageant. The Mormons are unconventional believers on every score, but especially because they stake their claim on the basis of being a new church, in a new age, in the New World.

One of the fundamental points of the Mormon faith is what is called Joseph Smith's first vision. Joseph Smith, Jr.—the name could not be more appropriate for someone who was to become prophet of a distinctively American variant of the Christian faith—gives an account of this event in a collection of brief writings entitled *The*

Pearl of Great Price, the title page of which refers to Smith as "first prophet, seer and revelator to the Church of Jesus Christ of Latter-day Saints." [1] Unusual as such a set of titles may be, it is not unusual as a religious affirmation, except perhaps in ascribing more powers to the founder than many religious leaders claim. In other words, one should not discount the authenticity of Joseph Smith as a religious leader on such grounds. Mohammed, for example, showed many times in the Koran that he was anxious about being thought a soothsayer, and the New Testament reports that Jesus was ridiculed by people who knew him and his family, presumably because he claimed a special relation with God, whom he called his father.

Like Mohammed, Joseph Smith remarks on the lack of distinction of his family. He was, he says, "an obscure boy," born in Sharon, Vt., in December 1805. His father moved the family to western New York when his namesake was "in my tenth year, or thereabouts." [2] The family lived in Palmyra for about four years, then moved to Manchester, in the same county. Smith's first vision is said to have taken place in the spring of 1820, when he was still fourteen. In 1823, by this account, he received three visits from the godly messenger Moroni, and then, after vain attempts to recover from the experience, he was shown the hillside place and the hidden plates. He was forbidden to remove them, however, but he returned each year to the same spot to meet the celestial messenger. It was not until 1827, Smith writes, that he was allowed to take the plates. He copied some of them in order to make a translation, but they were soon reclaimed by Moroni and became accessible no longer.

The first vision is an account of the appearance to Joseph Smith of "two Personages, whose brightness and glory defy all description." One calls him by name and, indicating the other, declares, "This is My Beloved Son. Hear Him!" They come to Smith when he is in the midst of great indecision over which church to join. The vision follows a classic pattern. In great doubt, Smith peruses the Bible and finds one verse particularly significant. For him it is the fifth verse of the first chapter of the Epistle of James: "If any of you lack wisdom, let him ask of God, that giveth to all men liberally, and upbraideth not; and it shall be given him." He goes to the woods to pray, feels great alarm and the fear of abandonment to dark powers, and suddenly is overcome with the light within which the two figures appear. He asks them the question that has been

1. See footnote 4, page 12. See the introductory pages of *The Book of Mormon* for an account of how it was given to Joseph Smith.

2. There are other autobiographical fragments in *The Pearl of Great Price* and historical details in *The Doctrine and Covenants.*

troubling him, and he is told to join none of the sects (he means by this the various Protestant denominations that have been competing for his attention) "for they are all wrong." [3] Their problem is that they have mistaken human ideas for the commandments of God, and they pay only lip service to the Lord. Smith is forbidden to pay attention to the competing sects, and the account closes with the cryptic remark that he was also told other things that he could not reveal at that time.

One of the most interesting things about the Mormon faith is that it is born and grows up right before our eyes, so to speak, and the doubts and perplexities of the sceptical can be fed by more palpable evidence than is usually available. There are, for example, a number of interesting parallels between the vision of Mohammed and the origins of Islam and the corresponding events in the beginnings of the Latter-day Saints, but what "really" happened in seventh-century Arabia is simply impossible to discover. In the case of Joseph Smith and the religious group on which he put his mark, there is room for considerable doubt. In the first place, the account of the early visions is written more than a decade after the last of them; the text itself announces that Smith wrote it in 1838, after the fledgling church had been moved from Kirtland, Ohio, to a place called Far West, Missouri, and when Smith was much preoccupied with questions of organization and authority. Moreover, although the account affirms that the first vision caused much controversy and was established very early as one of the pillars of the faith, along with belief in the divinity of Christ, references to the vision in the records of the decade before it was written about are said to be very few. Possibly after the church had become a going concern, the importance of the first vision was read back into the early record.

Similarly, the account of the giving of the Book of Mormon is difficult to accept at face value. Joseph Smith was not a learned man, nor did he claim to be; the difficulty therefore is that a reader is asked to believe the story entirely on the authority of divine intervention. It is interesting that Mohammed too felt himself to be an unlearned man favored by God as the recipient of a scripture intended for the people he lived among, the sacred book they needed to have. But the means of communication he described were simpler; the original of the Koran was written in heaven, and Mohammed was told by the divine messenger to recite what was dic-

3. See footnote 4, page 12.

tated to him. Thus he was not the author but only the spokesman for God, a prophet as Joseph Smith was to be after him. But in the case of the Book of Mormon, the text was buried on an undistinguished hillside by a member of a race not known in any other historical source. The text is no longer available; even now that the persecution is past that once justified its being returned to the custody of spiritual beings, there is no suggestion that the text will be found again. Even Joseph Smith was privileged to see it for only a short time. He needed supernatural assistance in order to translate it. What he was shown on the hillside was not only the plates but a breastplate in which were set the Urim and the Thummim, stones said to be the emblems of seers in former times. In the history of the Israelites of the Old Testament, these objects were part of the ritual adornment of priests. They may have been stones for the casting of lots by divine direction, though this is not certain. They are not mentioned when the Bible is telling about seers or people who had supernatural insight into the will of God.

To put it very simply, the faith of Mormons depends to a considerable degree on faith in the credibility of Joseph Smith. The amount of faith required is greater than that required by most other scriptural traditions. The text Smith gave his followers does not commend itself as the truth. To be sure, it makes reference to the biblical record at some points, but in the same manner as a historical novel might. It is indeed plausible that that is just what it is—a text written by a clergyman and submitted for publication but never reaching print until prepared under Smith's direction.[4] Since the evidence is only as good as Joseph Smith's testimony, the controversy in which his church was involved in its early years was largely over whether the golden plates actually existed, what was inscribed on them, and what evidence Smith had copied from them. Is it true that the texts, which are really the original sources of the Mormon scriptures as far as conventional scholarship is concerned, were actually the same as a version of ancient Egyptian writing and correctly translated by him? The texts themselves not being available, the critical mind has to be doubtful, and even one's faith is somewhat strained to accept this as truth. Since the Mormon Church has a powerful commitment to the acceptance of Joseph Smith's revelations, it would seem that the weakness of the evidence would long ago have destroyed this group. Yet its rapid growth and con-

4. Charles Braden gives the essentials of the case regarding *The Book of Mormon* in Chapter 13 of *These Also Believe* (New York: Charles Scribner's Sons, 1949).

tinued vitality argue otherwise. Has the church simply managed to silence all doubt? Could a fiction be established as fact on so large a scale?

MORMON UNITY

In answer, it must be said that the Latter-day Saints have been jealous of their possessions, which their isolated position in Utah helped them to protect. The church has not opened all of its archives, and only recently has an intellectual tradition for the discussion of the basis of Mormon faith been allowed to come into being even modestly. But again, it is important to ask whether this issue is after all the one that matters most. Nowadays people who are not Mormons are much less hostile than indifferent to the claims of the faith, and though the question of its credibility may at some future date make difficulties for the group, that moment has not yet arrived. In fact, one must ask himself what the real attraction of the church is, because people are joining it in great numbers, even though they are asked to believe and accept more than what is asked of members of other denominations. People are joining the church, and they are willing in turn to tell others what they have found in it. Undoubtedly the strong missionary emphasis has a lot to do with the success of the Mormon faith today.

Thus the credibility of the faith is less important than the act of believing. In fact, there is some evidence in social psychology that believing in what is difficult to verify commonly draws the believers more closely together, at least so long as what they are asked to believe is not obviously false. The further the original events fade into the past, the less focus there is on whether they are true, and the more attention is devoted to their outcome and the present functions of the organization. When the followers of Joseph Smith were forming a new church in the 1830's, to a considerable degree Smith was the issue with his new scriptures and his claim to be a "revelator"—that is, to be chosen to receive messages directly from God himself for delivery to his people.

Soon afterwards, however, Smith was dead, shot by a mob that broke into the jail at Carthage, Ill., on June 27, 1844, and killed him and his older brother Hyrum as they were awaiting trial on charges stemming from the Mormon government of the city of Nauvoo. The *Doctrine and Covenants,* the third authoritative book of the faith, contains rather fulsome praise of Smith after his martyrdom, comparing him with Jesus Christ in his work of salvation, but this source also seems to regard the murder as a necessary sealing of the work with the blood of the founder.[5] By this time the group is well established, vigorously evangelizing and gaining converts under the strong leadership of Brigham Young. Now the group has become the issue, and how it sustains itself is the vital issue, rather than the defense of Joseph Smith.

Let us look then at the group rather than the extraordinary man who founded it. Some elements of its story are familiar, in particular the forced migration of the main group of its people, who finally settled in the area of the Great Salt Lake, a place that was so barren that they realized they were not likely to be envied for it. There the church flourished, its people leading a strikingly independent existence that included the notorious institution of "plural marriage," by which men were allowed more than one wife, by consent of all the women involved if they followed the practice sanctioned by the church. The church was a communal organization as well, with an important voice in the politics and the economics of the region, and this seemed to violate the constitutional principle of the separation of church and state which was law in the states of the Union. Needless to say, Mormons were a scandal to freedom-loving nineteenth-century America.

What is less familiar is that the Mormon faith is a logical outcome of some of the major trends in the religious development of the prior two centuries in America. Western New York was what historians commonly call "the burned-over district." [6] Full of transplanted New Englanders, it had repeatedly been swept by revival fervor, much of which now was past. Significant in the account of Joseph Smith's first vision is what he is clearly rejecting. His family have become Presbyterians, but the Methodists and Baptists are also contending for his allegiance. He tells of how he related to a Methodist clergyman the circumstances of the meeting with the divine personages, only to be met with derision and contempt. No matter what the facts are about the vision, this reaction on the part of the clergyman is an accurate reflection of the historical situation. In its attempts to gain adherents, the Mormon faith competed directly with the evangelical denominations, particularly the Methodists and the Baptists, but also with important elements of the Presbyterian Church. These churches were developing the techniques used in revivals from that day to this, and they were reaching

5. The murder of Joseph Smith and his brother Hyrum in 1844 is interpreted in Section 135 of *The Doctrine and Covenants*.

6. See Whitney R. Cross, *The Burned-Over District* (New York: Harper and Row, Publishers, Inc., 1965).

people who were no longer being reached by the older churches of the colonial era.

Why were the traditional churches failing? The Congregationalists, the Episcopalians, and the more doctrinal Presbyterians based the authority of their teaching and practice on the Bible, but the Bible as interpreted by a learned clergy, men who often were content to mix socially with only the supposedly better class of people in their towns. These clergymen had lost touch, or perhaps had never been in touch, with the common man. For many such clergy with their university education, science and reason had come to have a credibility equal to and even higher than the Bible. So they preached reason and a rational morality. Finally, they tended to think of themselves as settled pastors of settled towns, ministers to the sober citizens rather than evangelists to those who were out of touch with the churches.

In addition, the theological ideas on which the older established doctrines were based made it difficult to reach ordinary people. Grace, which was the power of God ardently sought as the means of becoming justified in His sight in spite of your sinfulness, came to you only at God's intiative, and came only to those whom He favored. You could do nothing yourself, absolutely nothing, to deserve or to earn this reward. To a theologian, the reasons for these ideas make good psychological sense, but they are difficult to communicate to common people, and in practical terms they can be successfully employed only in what is truly a church—that is, a religious group to which all members of a community belong. When there are many religious groups, of course, each one is tempted to concentrate on the reasons why it is better than the others; the very act of choosing to join one rather than another implies that the individual can do a lot on his own behalf in religious terms. He can join one group or proclaim that his mind is his own church, as Thomas Paine did. Or, like Joseph Smith, he can reject all groups and start his own.

By contrast to the older churches, the Methodists and Baptists were among the more tolerant groups, no doubt because they knew they were good at winning people away from the older denominations. For them, the old predestinarian ideas had given way, or were fast giving way, to the conviction that you must be born again, and that you can be born again if the right means are used in a revival service. As has been mentioned previously, the Methodists developed a doctrine of perfectionism, which was a program of improving yourself morally and spiritually after conversion, with at least the theoretical possibility of becoming perfect. The Methodists also had a strong corps of traveling preachers on regular circuits, effective messengers for their version of the faith, even when they settled down and the camp meetings became annual conventions rather than revivals. The Baptists offered the particular advantage of independence to each local church, which could ordain as a preacher anyone who seemed to have a gift for communicating the Word of God. A good knowledge of standard biblical texts and a strong sense of effectiveness in the rhetoric of spiritual sincerity increasingly became requisites for success among the Baptists.

There were many people, however, who were still uncomfortable with the disproportionate stress placed on an emotional conversion experience by the revival denominations and on the necessity of imagining themselves the blackest of sinners beforehand if the conversion experience were to have its greatest effect. Such people had had enough of revivals, and yet they were no longer an audience for the teaching and preaching of the traditional clergy. To the poorly educated, the not-too-successful, and the dissatisfied, the Mormon faith provided a new combination of many of the elements of the evangelical faiths, plus the distinctive emphasis of a revelation specifically directed to the New World. For the story of the Book of Mormon told how the resurrected Christ made an appearance on this side of the "large waters," among the righteous people called the Nephites, who then lost their power when they fell away from the faith and were exterminated by their ancient enemies, the Lamanites, who also rejected Christ after a brief period of righteousness and became the people known in America as Indians.[7] Thus the Mormon faith is a recovery not only of lost records but of the lost faith of a once holy people in these regions. The European settlers, who thought of themselves as Christians, deceived themselves by following the teachings of men, with the result that they were called Gentiles by the texts of the Mormons, and their faiths were rejected.

MORMON PRACTICE

In practice, however, the Mormon faith takes to a logical conclusion many of the tendencies long operative in the older groups, and it gives in its day-to-day existence anything but the bizarre impression that Joseph Smith's history might suggest. For example, the account of his first vision is a kind of catechism for new converts, the theme of many a sermon, and a truth that must be accepted before

7. See, for example, 126–13 in *The Book of Mormon*.

baptism. Yet the conventional interpretation does not stress supernatural elements, the experience as an experience. It is not an ecstasy but a factual event. It is used as proof that God hears and answers the prayers of those who seek for answers. The presence of two figures in the vision is considered proof that Christ and God are two separate individuals, as against the conception of the Trinity in traditional Christian teaching. And the opposition to it is evidence of the work of Satan in resisting the truth. There is little if any evidence that this was how Joseph Smith himself used the story. Therefore it is plausible to infer that these uses of it serve the purposes of the later Mormon Church, which intends to make the faith as practical and concrete as possible.

Thus for Mormons God is a hard fact, a material body even as all things are, though this rarefied spiritual substance is apparent only to those who are themselves spiritual. God answers prayers; He rewards righteousness and punishes wrongdoing. He is a dependable spiritual resource. He has revealed what he wants man to do, and man will prosper in obedience to the divine will if he tries hard enough. To illustrate how this works in practice, here is a description of a typical Sunday worship service in a Mormon church. It must be said, first of all, that church buildings are heavily used by Mormons, especially in Utah, where they are centers for comprehensive social programs as well as religious meetings. In an outlying area, where the church is newly planted, the activity may be confined to Sundays, but the congregation takes its work seriously.

On one Sunday morning in such a church in a New England town, the eleven o'clock service (the conventional worship hour in most Protestant churches) was instead a time of religious education for adults as well as children. The parking lot was full of cars, and inside was a busy murmur of many classes in session. The importance of these classes is their relevance to the process of one's life in the church. After being baptized as an infant, the child of Mormon parents is confirmed at about age eight, which is early by conventional Protestant standards but about the same as a Catholic first communion. After confirmation, however, the Mormon faith offers its male members a unique set of obligations and opportunities. It is not that everyone needs to be converted, but that everyone shall be a priest—not in the figurative Lutheran sense but literally. There are two degrees of priesthood, that of Aaron and that of Melchizedek. Both are biblical in reference, though not as a sequence in this way. The Mormon boy becomes an Aaronic priest at about fourteen, or the time when most Protestants are confirmed. But in the Mormon case you are qualified as a priest to participate in worship services and thus to take a real part in the religious life of your congregation. Later, after high school, you are required to spend two years in a mission situation, at your own expense or your family's, and two young men from Utah were present as teachers in this church. Mormons also tithe—that is, give ten percent of their income to the church—so that it is obvious that to be a Mormon is to give an unconventional proportion of effort to your church. The second order of priesthood is required for officers such as elders and presidents of larger administrative units. One gets the impression that most Mormons are willing to work to get ahead, and that this sentiment is expressed in their church life just as in the affairs of every day.

In the evening, when the worship service was scheduled, the small meeting room filled well before the hour set for the service. A girl played classical tunes on the electric organ on one side, and babies and small children stayed with their parents throughout the service; no one seemed to mind it much when they chortled or cried as the room grew stuffy. At the opposite side from the organ console at the front of the room, two young men sat behind a table on which lay the utensils for the sacrament. Two or three rows of seats rose behind a low wooden screen facing the congregation. In the center was a lectern with a microphone, and before it several dishes of brilliant zinnias and marigolds. Otherwise the neatly modern room was devoid of decorations, ornaments, or symbols of any kind.

Similarly, and despite the richly imaginative historical narrative so conspicuous to an outsider, the Mormon liturgy is extremely simple. It is conducted by the men of the congregation, each taking his turn. A hymn is sung from a book in which tunes that would be familiar to any Methodist or other evangelical Protestant alternate with those produced by Mormon poets and composers, beginning with Joseph Smith's widow. The bishop, who is simply the presiding officer of the ward or local district congregation, gives an invocation of a thoroughly conventional sort. He asks the two men at the side of the room to preside over the sacrament, which they do as at every ordinary service. The sacramental elements are bread and water (rather than wine or grape juice), and they are given only as reminders of the work of Christ. Another hymn is sung, and at the end of the service a final hymn is sung and a benediction is spoken—again, as assigned by the bishop in a very informal way. Between the last two hymns and taking up the bulk of the time devoted to worship is a succession of three speakers who, again, are not specially trained leaders but ordinary people, members of the congregation who are encouraged to take their turn.

The speaking is strongly moral in tone. An attractive high school girl talks about service, using as her text the story of the Good Samaritan from the Gospel according to St. Luke. She gives many examples from ordinary life situations and works in at the end a quotation from the Book of Mormon. Next an older man, obviously not used to public speaking and apologetic about his theme, speaks about "the hand of God in the history of the early church," meaning of course the Latter-day Saints. He recounts in halting tones the story of Joseph Smith's first vision, the papers in his hands trembling a bit from his nervousness. No one seems to mind, but instead all listen attentively, for all have had the same experience or anticipate having it. The man closes with a reference to the famous "sea gull miracle." He presents in a somewhat sceptical tone the story of how, when the Mormon settlers in the valley of the Great Salt Lake were eagerly awaiting their first crop—the food that would take them through the long winter to come—a swarm of voracious locusts threatened to eat everything and doom them to starvation. Suddenly a flock of sea gulls, hundreds of miles from the Pacific, appeared, devouring the locusts and saving the crop. The speaker points out that though you might explain this as natural occurrence, for him the story shows the effect of the hand of God in the history of the church.

The final speaker is a handsome and forceful man, not a member of the congregation (the ward) but a representative of the president of the next higher unit, called the stake (in the Episcopal church this would be roughly the same as the diocese). He brings greetings and then enters his own plea for the moral life, particularly for sexual morality and the sanctity of family life. As a former Air Force pilot stationed in the Far East, he tells stories of how Oriental parents would offer their children for sale to American servicemen, and relates how the licentiousness of a serviceman that leads to an illegitimate child is evidence that sexual laxity causes us to hate our children. This is not just the morality of what is so glibly called "middle America," but something that runs considerably deeper. The Mormons have a number of unique ceremonies that must be performed in one of the temples of the church if they are to be performed at all. Until the completion of the largest of them, a building in Washington, D.C., the only temples in the United States have been in the Far West, which means that for many Mormons the rites require special trips. One such ceremony is eternal marriage, by which a couple are wedded for all time, in heaven as well as on earth. On the basis of a New Testament verse, Mormons are baptized on behalf of the dead; as a result the Mormons maintain perhaps the finest genealogical records anywhere, so that members of the church may bring ancestors into the church. The temple services are regarded as "sealing" relations that are soundly established here on earth, including the linking by eternal bonds of families that on earth are related "only" by marriage. Mormons do not seem to long to renounce enjoyment of this flesh but instead to build from a sure foundation in this life a structure that will never fall.

MORMON STRENGTH

What appears from this account is that the strength of the Mormon faith lies not nearly so much in its distinctive ideas as in the practices that knit the group strongly together. There is a democratic tendency in the worship of the church in that everyone participates rather than being ruled symbolically by a religious foster father. This democracy at the local level is combined with a strongly centralized authority system at the upper levels, so that the organization as a whole can be efficiently directed.

The central authority of the church is anchored in the belief that Joseph Smith was "revelator," empowered to communicate the will of God. This power has been passed down to the First Presidency, a patriarchal office exercised for life by very old men, a fact that may give the church what seems to outsiders and to some of its members an unduly conservative cast, but that also confirms faith in the family relations on which the church is built. This power of institutionalized revelation was exercised by Joseph Smith to initiate the Mormon custom of "plural marriage," or polygamy, and was later used also to abolish it in 1890 by the then president Wilford Woodruff, when it was important to establish better relations with the nation for Utah to receive admission as a state.[8]

It is probable that only a revelation through a new president would resolve one of the issues that has caused much criticism of the church—the prohibition of the various levels of the priesthood to black people. The Book of Mormon, like many other scriptures, considers dark color a mark of unrighteousness, but in practical terms it is probably the importance of kinship relations among Mormons that has kept the church from moving with the times on this issue.

All in all, the success of the Mormon faith probably depends most on its ability to create strong social bonds among straight-

8. See *The Doctrine and Covenants*, pp. 256–57.

forward people, mainly of Anglo-Saxon background, who value the traditional American virtues of honesty, morality, hard work, and a second chance for those who have slipped morally but are determined to mend their ways. Critics of it as a religion compare it with the ancient theological and ecclesiastical traditions of Europe, as they are represented in American churches, and can make a good case for seeing the Mormon faith as much less subtle, its theology somewhat questionable, and its rituals somewhat narrow. But this is not the only possible comparison, and it is probably not the most useful. Compared with the masonic orders, for example, there is the same fraternal appeal, the same devotion to social service, and the same sense of belonging to a spiritual group based on secret knowledge of truths unknown to outsiders. But there is also a more credible religious grounding in a Christianity that really has its roots in America.

In fact the communal aspects of the Mormon faith have had a more than simply spiritual or ecclesiastical basis almost from the beginning. In theology Joseph Smith took the old idea of the covenant, which meant an agreement graciously entered into by God because he wished to show favor on his chosen people despite their unworthiness, and transformed it into a contract by which God was bound as long as people did what they promised (see *Doctrine and Covenants* 82:8–10). In effect, the Mormons gave a new interpretation to the old image of the keys of the kingdom, which meant the power to open the doors of heaven and therefore accomplish the heavenly intention, a power that in Roman Catholic theory is vested in the Pope, the successor of Peter, but in Protestant churches has been the mystical outcome of the cooperation between the church as the body of Christ and Christ as its head. In Mormon texts, this power is variously committed to Joseph Smith, to men on earth, and to the Presidency of the High Priesthood of the Church. The important point is that there is little if any mystery about the ways in which God and man are related, and that Latter-Day Saints, by due obedience to the revealed law of their sacred texts and their community, can inherit the earth and the world to come.

This spiritual confidence is reflected in some other distinctive aspects of Mormon faith and practice. On the one hand, Mormons are millennialists, believing strongly in the imminent return of Jesus Christ after mankind undergoes a period of tribulation and a day of judgment. Like many other groups that similarly have drawn their original followers from relatively underprivileged and undereducated people, they have seen themselves as destined to be vindicated by this expected catastrophe and transformed by their righteousness into a favored group of agents of godly rule. But the concreteness of the Mormon vision has combined this image of a supernatural fulfillment with a faith that the kingdom of God is already present in their church. The ruling Council of Twelve is constituted of living apostles, commissioned as were their forerunners in the time of the Old World Jesus to "preach the Gospel to all nations." There is also speculation that there was in the old Mormon country of the Utah Territory a secret Council of Fifty, which was a kind of provisional government of the kingdom of God, ready to step into power when the occasion arose.[9] Some think that when the issue of statehood arose, the issue of polygamy was only the lurid cover for the constitutional issue posed by a too close connection between the church and the real governing power of the Mormon Territory.

The chief administrators of the Church of Jesus Christ of Latter-Day Saints, in other words, have a real power in the church that exceeds that of the leaders of any other Protestant group of comparable size. (Recent estimates of the total membership of the church in America exceed 3 million, a figure that would place Mormons very close to the Presbyterians and Episcopalians.) In theory, at least, their power is in some respects greater than that of the Pope, who may speak authoritatively for the Catholic Church only under highly restrictive conditions of canon law. And, of course, in Utah the influence of the Mormon Church is powerful because of this structure of authority and because the majority of citizens belong to it and contribute heavily to its work. It is difficult to determine, however, how deeply this power extends into the day-to-day lives of people and into the current economic and political structures even of that still unique region of America. One would expect the evangelical origins of the faith to manifest themselves in a greater concern for moral issues and a moral interpretation of economic and political life and not so much in direct intervention into such areas. One would expect the memory of the early communal economic life to have yielded to new realities. To a degree these expectations have been fulfilled; in fact, Mormons have become some of the most dedicated advocates of economic free enterprise. It is not likely that Utah could again become a theocratic state, if indeed it ever was, yet "Mormon country" remains unique.

To Mormons in other areas of America and the world, as we have said, the faith presents itself alongside many competitors, in a situ-

9. For more information on the Council of Fifty, see Klaus J. Hansen, "The Metamorphosis of the Kingdom of God," *Dialogue* I, 3 (Autumn, 1966), 63–83.

ation somewhat resembling what Joseph Smith faced a century and a half ago. But by contrast to many of those other faiths, it is more active, presenting a truth seen not as shrouded in ancient mystery but ever-present, straightforward, and perhaps even homespun, a bulwark to the hard but righteous life of virtue. It requires much of its people, in regular attendance, learning, tithing, and the duty of making a mission, but the corresponding rewards are great in a sense of self-worth and the support of a warmly committed community of believers who help you do your best. This mutuality of support by members of the church, together with their continued acceptance of some extraordinary beliefs and an unusual institutional structure, places Mormons still among the unconventional believers. There is little indication of an early change in this identity.

Minorities
and Unconventional Belief

"That is the Sun. You are meeting your Father the Creator for the first time. You must always remember and observe these three phases of your Creation. The time of the three lights, the dark purple, the yellow, and the red reveal in turn the mystery, the breath of life, and warmth of love." [1]

Such words strike us much more poignantly than would have been the case even in our parents' times, for it is only in the light of more recent historical experience that we have begun to take a new look at our past, to reexamine the assumptions that ruled our thinking, and to reevaluate what was done in the name of the manifest destiny of our nation. Often, to be sure, such reexamination consists of exercises in futility, not only because what was done cannot be undone, but because it is wrong to judge the past from the standpoint of insights that only hard experience has given us. It was not so long ago, after all, that we went to war in Europe under the leadership of one of our most conscientious presidents with the idealistic belief that it was our obligation to make the world safe for democracy.

But we do need to be reminded that people were living here before the great waves of immigration washed away so many marks of their culture, and that they too were religious people. Yet Indian

1. Frank Waters, *The Book of the Hopi* (New York: Ballantine Books, Inc., 1963), pp. 6–7.

peoples like those from whose creation myth the words above are taken were considered to be a menace by most European settlers. Particularly from the point of view of the Christianity of the time, the Indians were marked as pagans whom one was obligated to attempt to convert before their souls were condemned to hell fire. Lately we have begun to value many of the Indians' religious attitudes and particularly their sense of the need to live in harmony with natural forces and in fellowship with the animals they depended on for survival. True, we should resist romanticizing Indian cultures, for not all of them encouraged people to live peacefully with each other. It is only that in contemporary times, after insistent minority voices have been raised, the nation as a whole has begun to appreciate their values and patterns of feeling, which were hardly noticed before and, if noticed, were often heedlessly disregarded.

Indians, Mexican-Americans (Chicanos), Orientals, and any of a host of people of non-European lineage or non-Western religious traditions have always had to recognize the fact that they were disregarded and despised by many of the European groups that had become established in the United States. Often there was a kind of unself-conscious and even sometimes a genial snobbery about this, since it seemed obvious a century or so ago that European civilization was the crown of a long process of human progress and was intended by God to bring a higher form of life to all. Peoples not yet blessed with the many benefits due eventually to come to them were not regarded as oppressed except by poverty, lack of education, and governments not yet enlightened by Western ideals.

It is only lately, of course, that we have focused a harsh light on our own cultural values and found them not so preeminent after all. We may have gone too far in the opposite direction in recent years; but even if we recover some of our old optimism about the quality of our culture, we are not likely to ignore again the cultural identities of the conspicuously different minorities among the general population. In most cases these cultural identities are confirmed and symbolized by distinctive religious traditions. In fact, it may be that we can assess the strength and durability of minority cultural identities more accurately through assessment of the state of their religious institutions than in any other way.

The Indian case is interesting because it accompanies all our history and enlivens such fundamental myths as those of the pioneer and the cowboy. In countless stories the western pioneer learns the wisdom of nature from the Indian in the wilderness, while the cowboy fights him to protect the herd. But by far the most important question is the question of the minority group that is the most conspicuous and at the same time the largest, the Negroes. The religious trials of blacks are in many ways a reflection of their struggles to discover a workable identity in the midst of a society that has always been ready to treat them as aliens. It may well be that the religious forms that blacks choose in years to come will be the best indication of their relation to the mainstream of American life.

The religion of minority groups has an important place in a book about unconventional religion in America, because from the viewpoint of the majority, all such religion is unconventional religion, since it consists of beliefs and practices different from what most people are used to in their religious institutions. But of course the viewpoint of the majority is not the only perspective. What we discover from it are some general differences between the two groups —the majority and the minority—but we need to press further if we are to have any idea how the members of the minority groups look in their own eyes and how they differ among themselves. "They all look the same to me" is an old expression of white ignorance about black people. When we become more knowledgeable, we discover that whites may analyze black culture just as they do that of the majority population and find many of the same kinds of differences within it, even granted the general differences between blacks and whites. In particular, the difference between conventional and unconventional believers is an important key to the meaning of what has lately come to be called the "black experience," and it is probably just as important a key to what the future holds for race relations in American society.

How are we to distinguish between conventional and unconventional religion among blacks? We may do as we do with other groups, by discovering what the ordinary, the expected form of participation is, and what the differences are between that and groups which are self-consciously new and different. Black people, in the first place, are at least as involved in religious practice as any other group in the general population. Blacks go to church in about the same numbers, and they care at least as much about the problems of their faith and its relation to daily living. It is also true that there are at least a few blacks in almost every organized religious group. In some cases there are specific historical reasons for this. For example, the Moravians, a German group whose cultural center is Bethlehem, Pa., have always had a strong commitment to missionary work. One of the centers of this work was in the Caribbean region; thus West Indian immigration to New York City in recent times brought many blacks into the few Moravian churches in the metropolitan area, and it may well be that their participation in this small religious family could be related to a desire to distinguish themselves from black people of American lineage.

In other groups, of course, the number of black members is disproportionately small. One church of black people is among the largest Episcopalian congregations in the United States, but overall the proportion of black members is much smaller in the Episcopal denomination. Only some five percent of Roman Catholics are nonwhites, although blacks make up a tenth or more of the total population of the country. Only a few blacks are Jewish although it is perhaps surprising that any are.[2] Similarly, one would not expect to find black members in the ethnic churches of the Russians or the Scandinavian Lutheran groups and the like. But since blacks are religious in about the same proportion as the rest of the population, their absence from many other white denominations is compensated for by the existence of almost exclusively black Protestant groups. Some of these groups have a rather long history; two major Methodist groups of black people were founded quite early in the nineteenth century, not long after the establishment of the denomination as an independent group in America. Other black churches date from the agony of the Civil War, before which several Protestant groups divided North and South and black and white, in some cases not ever to be rejoined.

CONVENTIONAL BLACK RELIGION

What, then, is the conventional religion of black people? It is a Protestant creed, but for good historical reasons it is located primarily within certain fairly well-defined limits. One reason is regional. The southeastern quarter of the country is the most heavily Protestant part, probably because it was not deeply involved in the heavy non-Protestant and non-Christian immigration of the turn of the last century. In addition, it must be emphasized that the Protestantism of the old South is overwhelmingly evangelical—belonging to groups whose identity was formed by ideas and methods like John Wesley's.

Indeed, Methodism is strong in the South, as one would expect, but even more conspicuous is the concentration of Baptists. One would expect these two denominations to include most black churchgoers, as they do, but two differences between the Methodist and Baptist churches provide convincing reasons why the Baptist faith

2. Gallup Opinion Index, "Special Report on Religion," February 1969.

has historically been the faith of the overwhelming majority of black Christians in the United States. In the first place, while the Methodist denomination is centrally organized, with emphasis on the clergy's riding "circuits" on horseback in the early days to cover all their congregations, each Baptist congregation is a self-governing unit in theory, and there is always a traditional opposition to movements toward centralized authority. Thus while some free blacks in New York City and Philadelphia felt they had to break with the Methodists to form their own churches, black Baptists always had the right to form and govern themselves.

Secondly, Baptist churches historically had also the right to choose their own clergymen, and since they were part of the evangelical revival tradition, they tended to choose men who had power to stir people—strong preachers who burned with the power of the spirit and were able to generate an emotional response. True, Methodists also worked in this way, preaching a strongly biblical gospel, interpreting sin and the powers of hell in concrete detail and making it possible for sinners to feel the releasing power of conversion and forgiveness and to confirm themselves in a moral life. But the Methodist clergy were a fraternity, inevitably more white than black, and the issue of slavery and race was never altogether absent. Thus the Baptist Church, and related organizations like the burial society and the credit union, were institutions which black people could control for themselves, and the ministry was one of the few directions an ambitious black man could take to advance himself to a position of authority. Often those who did find other means to success were expected to have the preacher's gifts as a speaker, the power to move a crowd, but in any case the black community retains a strong capacity to respond warmly to a powerful voice. Martin Luther King, Jr., himself the son of a preacher, was an outstanding example of this kind of leadership. He reached an audience far wider than the black community alone, but there are many others within the black community who approach him in the power to move people with Christian preaching.

Thus the conventional religion of blacks is strongly congregational and warmly enthusiastic Baptist worship. There is a degree of participation by all members of the congregation that is common to all revival groups to some extent, but notably absent from the more sedate worship of the conventional churches of white people. Let me describe one such worship service to indicate something of the quality of typical black religious experience. The setting is a converted theater on an urban street. In rural communities the building may be a modest wood frame structure; smaller, less well-known city congregations may well worship together in rented store fronts. On the whole, Baptist congregations of all persuasions tend to be rather smaller than groups of the other old denominations, which means that individual Baptist congregations are less often able to build and maintain impressive churches. On the other hand, there are many indications that poor people give more to their churches, in absolute terms, not only relative to income, than more prosperous people do. It is apparent, in this congregation as elsewhere, that the church receives the best from its people. The people are well dressed, and ushers clad in white direct worshipers to the rapidly filled pews. An electronic organ plays into a powerful sound system, so that everybody can hear what is said and sung.

It is important to underscore the vital role of music in this kind of worship. American popular music has again and again been influenced by the musical traditions of the black churches, and in turn has nourished them. Aretha Franklin and many other black singers of star status come from a church background. In the church we are now discussing, the choir fills the stage except for the podium and the preacher's chair. The singers have strong voices and use them expressively; they sway from side to side in time with the music, whose beat is insistent. Particularly well-sung phrases evoke shouts of appreciation from members of the congregation, especially when a soloist comes forward to the microphone and sings the "testifying," which has long been a feature of the worship of revival-oriented groups. The choir director steps out plainly to the middle of the crowded stage and conducts with an athletic vigor that would probably be frowned upon in white middle-class churches but is fully appropriate here. A dominant impression created by such worship, in fact, is strong feeling, but feeling that is more obviously corporate than in most services of worship, even in highly emotional ones. Evangelists, as has been stated previously, seem to thrive particularly by generating a sense of personal relationship with the many individuals who respond to them, but you rarely lose a sense that a gap remains, a space of psychological distance that neither party to the relation wishes to erase completely. In the black churches, by contrast, there is greater mutual involvement, constant or almost constant vocal interplay, a pervasive informality, and warmth of feeling. Shouts of "Yes" or "Amen. Say it, preacher!" punctuate the preaching, the singing, and the praying. If in some few individuals this gives way to a loss of emotional control—as happens, of course, in revival worship of all varieties—the group ministers to them with a tolerant friendliness difficult to match in any other social group.

The basis of this close communal life is a very traditional set of Christian ideas, to which the words of the songs, the prayers, and the preaching return again and again. We were in sin and misery, a prey to troubles and dangers on every hand, but perhaps most of all to our own weaknesses. Then Jesus came to bring us forgiveness and redemption and give us strength to carry on. Like us, everyone, no matter how high and mighty in this world, stands under the judgment of God, which Christ made known in his life among us. Because we know this truth, our lives are brought under control, we can shout for joy, and we can bear the very real burdens of the struggles against poverty and discrimination, and particularly, in these times on city streets, against the demonism of drugs.

OPIUM OF THE PEOPLE?

Such emphases in the life of a church raise a question that is particularly associated with the thinking of Karl Marx, the intellectual father of Communism, but that has become a general one among people who are concerned with whether religion is good for people and should be encouraged. Marx once wrote that religion is the opium of the people.[3] He did not mean that it had no reason for being; in fact, he felt that religion is a true reflection of how things actually are in the world. God is a father because fathers are like gods under the law and under certain sets of family customs. In many ways this is identical with the psychological line of argument taken by Sigmund Freud in our own century, except for the fact that Freud concentrated on personal relations and feelings, on the importance of the relations between fathers and sons in the generation of guilt rather than what Marx emphasizes, the role of religion in giving people an explanation of why they feel as miserable as they do. For Marx, quite simply, people feel miserable because they are in a miserable situation; in this respect, religion is altogether true to the extent that it can show people how truly miserable they are.

Where religion is false, for Marxist thinking, is in its solution to the problem. It is wrong, according to orthodox Marxists, whether it offers some kind of otherworldly paradise as a compensation for misery in this life, as traditional Christianity and Islam do, for example, or whether it affirms that the misery of the human condition is a problem incapable of solution, as do the older traditions

3. The basic text is Marx's "Contribution to the Critique of Hegel's Philosophy of Right," which can be found in *Karl Marx and Friedrich Engels on Religion* (New York: Schocken Books Inc., 1964).

of the religions of India—Hinduism and Buddhism. Marxism is a basically optimistic social philosophy—a social philosophy because although in many respects it acts like a religion, it refuses to offer a religious solution such as salvation; and optimistic because, unlike pessimistic religions or philosophies like existentialism, it affirms that the problem of human misery does have a solution in society. True, the solution demands radical or revolutionary means, because the whole point of recognizing misery in the world is to change the conditions that produce it. Religion, most Marxists have felt, gives up the fight far too easily. That is why it is called opium, a narcotic against reactions that otherwise would lead to necessary change, the kind of change that will result in the reduction of misery and the eradication of the feeling that human existence must inevitably be miserable in important respects.

Many people feel that the conventional religion of black people in America is very vulnerable to this argument, since it has concentrated so heavily on personal salvation and morality, on heavenly rewards rather than opposition to social injustice. The old movie "Green Pastures" is a good case in point with its image of God as a benevolent and elderly black gentleman presiding over a heavenly picnic and smoking a big cigar. In general, as we have already seen, these emphases are characteristic of the evangelical Protestant groups that converted black people, but the difference is that they are so much more dominant in the black community as to be typical of its religious life.

Does this mean that the conventional religion of black people is opium in the Marxist sense? As the songs says, "It Ain't Necessarily So." For one thing, opium in the Marxist sense is a metaphor, but opium in the form of heroin is a real narcotic in the community surrounding the church we have been describing. This church takes pride in being part of the fight against the drug traffic. Next door to it is its own store-front antinarcotic center directing attention particularly to teenagers. Its workers do their best to discover and put out of business local distributors of heroin, or at least to put them on the defensive. The clergyman preaches with great rhetorical force in terms of sin and the need for personal redemption, but he also gives his support to proposals to jail drug pushers for life. More importantly, perhaps, he has credentials in the field of social change. As a former associate with Martin Luther King, Jr., in the Student Christian Leadership Conference, he has many times put himself on the line in opposition to discrimination against black people. It may be argued that the civil rights movement in which Dr. King was so important was too traditional in aims and too moderate in methods, but what it achieved may be of more consequence in the real world than more radical impulses. In any case, the movement is evidence that social action can take place on the foundation of a traditional evangelical religious position. And the surviving speeches and sermons of Dr. King have an emotional force that few if any in the white world now command. This is true in large measure because King could draw on so much of the traditional Christian imagery and make use of it for a prophetic message of social justice that after all comes from the Scriptures and that doubtless lies in the background of Marx's social passion as well.

The civil rights movement of the 1960s provided an impulse to many blacks to start thinking more militantly about their situation in America. The movement probably made it easier for many blacks to become militant just because of its respectable religious sponsorship. As for any hard evidence as to whether religion hinders or helps blacks change the conditions under which they live, whatever evidence exists turns out to be rather inconclusive. Some members of the black community who are religious are less militant on civil rights issues than blacks in general are, while others turn out to be more militant. Perhaps the Marxist question does not need to be answered conclusively in any case—religious people would certainly say in most instances that there is more to religion than social revolution. More useful inferences may be drawn in the last analysis from the unconventional religion of black people, to the extent that it demonstrates not only the image of a painful situation and a wistful wish for change, but the presence of effective efforts to attain a change.

Who, then, are the unconventional believers among black people, and what kinds of religious groups have they been forming and joining? Civil rights activism is a relatively new phenomenon. It certainly does not even yet express what most blacks are thinking, but as we have seen, it has often taken place under quite conventional sponsorship. More recently, the sense of not being fully accepted members of American society has provided a justification to some blacks for joining the Black Panthers and other similar black activist groups or for styling themselves "urban guerillas," at war with the institutions of white society but particularly with its police. These groups involve very few people, but by their actions such people draw an inordinate share of the attention of the news media. They affect more conventional blacks by providing fascinating or horrifying images of violence; and it is difficult to assess the importance of this effect. More substantial evidence is the emergence of groups of unconventional believers who base their search for a new identity for blacks on rejection of European institutions and particularly Christianity, which they consider the faith that justified enslavement of their ancestors and systematically destroyed their culture.

Thus among some blacks there has been a vogue for African clothing, dance, hair styles, and personal ornamentation. The Swahili language has begun to be taught in a few city schools, and lately a turn-of-the-year festival called Kwanza has been proposed as a replacement for Christmas.[4] One discovers a considerable interest in voodoo, the old religion of ecstasy, magic, and demonic possession, which came to America with the slaves, secured a stronghold in Haiti, and lately emerged from what was probably a significant underground existence among black Americans to a position of more or less open practice in some cities. How much are such activities motivated by conscious opposition to or differentiation from conventional believing? It is difficult to know, and also difficult in some cases to find out, if you are white. What we require, therefore, is a substantial example of a group with an important place in contemporary black life, whose activities have been knowledgeably reported, but a group that is self-consciously engaged on a program to set blacks on a quest for a new religious identity.

THE NATION OF ISLAM

On the same city block as the Baptist Church already described, as it happens, is a very imposing building housing one of the most substantial outposts of a group whose official name is the Nation of Islam but is better known as the Black Muslims. Based in Chicago, the Black Muslim organization is well established in several major cities, in some of which it owns and administers considerable property. The central figure of the group is a man named Elijah Muhammad. It is he who is referred to by the name of the tabloid-sized newspaper *Muhammad Speaks,* which is sold on city street corners much as *Awake* and *The Watchtower* are sold by Jehovah's Witnesses, many of whom, by the way, also are black.

Just as the activity of selling newspapers is a mark of similarity with one group, so the type of organization may be the basis for an interesting comparison with another. The selling of newspapers is a source of revenue to help sustain a large communal enterprise; it is also, naturally, a means of advancing the point of view of the

4. See articles in *The New York Times* on several days in December 1972.

group, even among the white people whom Black Muslims are taught to regard as devilish. Such an activity also implies an authoritative voice and a centralized structure from which that voice will sound. It may be imagined, in addition, that communicating the message of the Nation of Islam to others, when advanced as a religious obligation, helps the many members of the sect who always require a clear sense of what they must do to be saved. All the members of Jehovah's Witnesses, by comparison, are called "publishers of the kingdom" because of their work as distributors of literature concerning the will of God. The Witnesses proclaim in this way the news of the imminent approach of the divine kingdom under the direct rule of Christ. This is not at all the point of view of the Black Muslims, who believe in a nation in this world, to be carved out of America and redistributed to the blacks who as slaves gave so much uncompensated labor that they have paid for such land many times over.

Similarly, it is interesting to compare the organization centered around Elijah Muhammad with a group of a generation ago that venerated a black man as its leader and made him the focal point of a network of ownership of considerable property, used in the service of the group. The former leader was called Father Divine. His following was concentrated in New York City and Philadelphia, but it appeared in many other places as "Father Divine's Peace Mission Movement." These outposts of the faith were known as "heavens," and they were noteworthy in a time of general economic depression before World War II for marvelously bountiful banquets at which guests both black and white were accorded a genuinely warm hospitality. The contributions of Father Divine's faithful made possible the purchase of many residences in crowded parts of cities, places where people of modest means lived safely and comfortably under a strict moral code and in deep devotion to their benevolent leader, who promised them that he could never die.[5]

Father Divine was certainly not a civil rights activist, and there is a lot of truth to the quasi-Marxist argument that his organization was a place of refuge from a situation that ought to have been changed rather than endured. But who can say that such a movement did not make at least an indirect contribution to the conditions out of which a more militant kind of consciousness grew? In any case, the contrast is interesting between Father Divine and Elijah Muhammad, and indeed between the former and other black

5. For more information on Father Divine, see the first chapter of Charles Braden, *These Also Believe* (New York: Charles Scribner's Sons, 1949).

leaders who are proclaiming that some version of Islam is a real religious option for them. Islam is a Third World religion, not involved in the power struggles between the nominally Christian West and the officially atheistic Communist powers. As such, it is in a position to profit from playing the great powers against each other. It is the predominant faith in many nonwhite countries, especially in newly independent and aggressively anticolonial nations across the northern half of Africa. Islam is based on a revelation that came after the revelation to the Jews and Christians, from the same God but to people for whom, according to Mohammed, those faiths were not really appropriate.

Being later in time, the revelation on which Islam is based has always been able to make the claim of finality against Christianity, much as Christianity made its claims against the religion of the Israelites. Islam also enshrines this revelation in an authoritative book, the Koran, whose presentation has the advantage of being more single-minded and often more clearly understandable than the Bible. Islam, finally, is a faith that teaches uprightness and moral self-discipline, with a clear set of religious requirements that are not unduly arduous but have the intention of inspiring a high standard of public and private responsibility. Significantly, it is not a faith that puts any premium on "enthusiasm." There are Moslem mystics and ecstatics, but the major stress in the community is on law and submission to the will of Allah. Believers are not expected to sing and shout about their need for salvation but quietly to do what is required of them and thus become people whom Allah favors.

All these features of the faith of Islam have some measure of advantage in the appeal to black people in contemporary America, especially to men. The more militant they come to be in their feelings about racial injustice, the more they are apt to see a great appeal in an alternative to the religious traditions of the people who have oppressed them, especially a faith that in the past fought many victorious battles against religious crusaders. Islam is a manly faith. It is straightforward and unemotional, although still carrying the respectability of being a religion based on scripture, with books to be studied and a message to be spread. Islam is also an uncompromising faith, and it can therefore engender in its adherents hatred against those outside the faith. On the other hand, it carries a universal appeal, not just a message to the Arabs, and thus it has been taken to heart by a wide variety of peoples from Morocco to Indonesia and from the Soviet Union to India. The duty of making a pilgrimage to Mecca once in every Moslem man's lifetime brings together an astonishing diversity of people under conditions that at least temporarily dissolve their differences.

The Black Muslims were originally brought together during the Depression by a man who called himself W. D. Fard.[6] Fard gathered his initial following by selling door to door and using these meetings as occasions for informing blacks of what he said was their true heritage. He said very little about where he came from, and many thought that he was an Arab rather than a Negro. The truth of the matter remains obscure, but it is clear that the teachings that set the course of future development of the movement started from what his hearers knew—the Bible and some knowledge of the Christian tradition—and turned them against themselves by identifying them with the white culture, which discriminated against blacks. An elaborate mythology was produced after a time, one that celebrated the past glories of dark people and came increasingly to denounce whites for having stolen and deceived their way to rule in the contemporary world, against the principles of true justice and manhood by which blacks lived. In fact, to be white came to be regarded by Black Muslims as to be lacking in color, therefore to be inherently weak and ripe for early destruction. From their own abundant experience of being victimized, and from an all-too-easily compiled catalogue of modern atrocities committed by whites, the Black Muslim preacher can make a good case for the inherent superiority of black people, at least to an entirely black audience whose solidarity depends on just such a view.

An expected consequence of this point of view is the repudiation of integration, since whites are said to be incapable of doing or being good. For their part the Black Muslims actively discourage white participation in their services, which nevertheless are occasionally televised. The temples in which services are held are closely guarded, not because they are shrines—intrinsically holy places—but more because of a strong sense of the need to defend the boundaries of the group against white intrusions or hostile criticism. This militant stance is in many respects realistic, since the short history of the group has been marked by many episodes of violence, including the assassination of Malcolm X, the dynamic leader who had risen rapidly to a position of leadership within the group but then repudiated it and began to erect a rival structure. A horrifying repetition of many aspects of Malcolm's experience took place early in

6. For more information on the Black Muslims, see E. U. Essien-Udom, *Black Nationalism* (New York: Dell Publishing Company, Inc., 1964). C. Eric Lincoln has also published a revised edition of his highly respected *The Black Muslims in America* (Boston: Beacon Press, 1973).

1973 with the murder of seven people, including five children, in a Washington, D.C., house given to a rival Moslem group by the basketball star Kareem Abdul-Jabbar. Like Malcolm, the leader of this group, Hamaas Abdul Khaalis, had been a rising leader among the Black Muslims before founding his own group. Though a statement from the headquarters in Chicago disavowed any connection with the murders, it remains all too plausible that *someone* did them in defense of what he took to be the true version of the faith.[7]

MARKS OF THE FAITH

Their militancy, defensiveness, and hostility toward whites remain some of the most obvious characteristics of Black Muslims and the chief issues to be considered in answering the question about the future of the group as an attractive religious option for American blacks. The reasons for its appeal to some are obvious enough—in its mythology it reverses the traditional relation of the two races and thus provides a strong foundation for self-respect for blacks who feel a powerful anger about their status in American society. Perhaps needless to say, this is particularly true for poor and uneducated blacks, especially black men uncomfortable with the emotionalism of conventional Baptist worship. The Black Muslims have gained many converts among the prison population, and they have vigorously recruited among the professional athletes—Mohammed Ali is a prominent example—who have done so much to enhance the self-respect of black people generally.

As another aspect of its separatist intentions, the Nation of Islam has raised an impressive structure of self-sufficient institutions to give its adherents education and opportunities for economic advancement. Its teachings are directed against some of the pervasive problems of ghetto communities—alcoholism, drug addiction, and broken families. The Black Muslim man becomes a worker and an exemplary family man, the acknowledged head of the family, whose wife dresses modestly, defers to his authority, and helps him teach their children self-respect and respect for the authority of the faith. Alcohol is forbidden to all Moslems, and their dietary rules are like those of the Jews, especially with respect to the avoidance of pork. For Black Muslims these rules are used to repudiate the old identity of the Southern rural slave or sharecropper, in whose diet pork was

7. See various newspaper and periodical articles for the first quarter of 1973.

a staple. As for distinctive styles of behavior, manliness of an aggressive variety is at once encouraged and controlled, in that Black Muslims arm themselves against expected attacks from whites but learn to avoid fighting and to be gentle and forgiving to their own, except perhaps those unwise enough to leave the group and criticize it in public. One of the proudest identities within the group is membership in the Fruit of Islam (FOI), a group chosen with care from among the fittest young men in every temple of the faith and trained both physically and psychologically to maintain the security and discipline of the membership. These men are organized into a quasi-military structure. They give the unmistakable impression that if any attack comes, they will be ready for it.

In a curiously ironic way, however, the Black Muslims have arranged things so as to be able to benefit from white culture without admitting it. Since they stress economic success, especially in setting up small businesses for their members or in farming tracts of land that they have been purchasing in the South, they are obviously in need of commercial expertise and the cooperation of white businessmen. Although Black Muslims consider these needs real ones, they acknowledge it to be no virtue in white people to be able to satisfy them, because the main strength of whites lies in the power to deceive blacks and steal from them. It is therefore only just retribution to take back from whites the skills and property that blacks should have by right. With some such secret motive the Black Muslim faithful can be model employees and willing subordinates.

These considerations suggest some very deep contradictions in the movement, however, tensions that have become the source of rather considerable difficulties. In the first place, one criticism of the Nation of Islam is that it seems primarily economic and political in its orientation rather than religious. It is certainly true, for example, that no obviously religious tone dominates the Black Muslim worship services. They consist largely of long discourses in the general framework of the group's theology, delivered by a leader to an attentive audience segregated by sex and unmoving and quiet except for a responsive "That's right," or some such occasional phrase from a listener. This recalls the Baptist service, but little else does. On the other hand, the worship of some other groups is likewise simple and given over to addresses proportionately much longer than the conventional sermon. Mormon worship is an example. The Black Muslims have largely rejected traditional black religious enthusiasm, but Islam *is* a relatively simple faith in this respect. Black Muslims can scarcely be faulted for propagating a faith that convinces many blacks that it can lift them out of an intolerable condition and put them into effective contact with a proud tradition.

It is here that the major problem lies, because the relationship between the doctrine of Elijah Muhammad, present leader of the Black Muslims, and that of traditional Islam is difficult to reconcile at two points in particular. In the first place, racism is foreign to Islam, and many Moslem leaders are uncomfortable with the racial exclusiveness of the American group. Secondly, Elijah Muhammad claims more importance for his role as what he calls a "messenger of Allah" than is easily accommodated to the tradition that Mohammed, founder of the faith in the seventh century, was the last of the prophets of God. Important defections from the group take place on these issues and give substance to the implication that the group defines itself too negatively to be long credible as an authentic religion. It is difficult to say, since it cannot be safely predicted that the alienation of large numbers of young black men will cease to find expression in such a faith.

Perhaps the most telling indication of the force of persuasion that the various forms of Islam can exert on young and impatient blacks is the practice of changing names. Elijah Muhammad was born Elijah Poole, and Hamaas Abdul Khaalis was Ernest Timothy McGhee; as is well known from the sports pages, Cassius Clay adopted the Moslem name of Mohammed Ali, and Abdul-Jabbar was Lewis Alcindor. Many people, of course, have changed their names in the process of adopting an American identity, but this is usually a matter of Anglicizing or simplifying the spelling or the sound. The Black Muslims make a more serious point of adopting the letter X as a last name in many cases, underscoring the fact that most black people in America have names given them arbitrarily when their slave ancestors were emancipated. Of all American minorities, only blacks had to make the leap into full partnership in American life without benefit of a traditional culture, or even names of their own.

The Nation of Islam therefore represents a contemporary effort to make good those losses. Its future success depends to a considerable degree on the success of integration, but since the movement identifies so heavily with traditional Islam, it will probably be forced to make its peace with the conventional religion of Moslem countries. In doing so it will lose some appeal for alienated American blacks. If at the same time blacks have made economic and social gains, a less militant Islam will be in a position of competition with modernized versions of the conventional religion of black people, so that Islam too will have the look of a conventional faith and may survive on that basis. Islam, after all, sees itself as a near relative of both Judaism and Christianity. For the moment, however, the Black Muslims are a dynamic organization and an unconventional religious possibility for blacks. If it is true, as seems likely, that a sense of being victimized, rather than an impulse toward some kind of salvation, drives most members into the group, the existence of the group remains a powerful reality in American society, so that future changes in the group depend more on general social trends than is probably the case for other religious groups.

THE FAITH OF BLACK MILITANCY

It is not surprising that Black Muslims have prospered in a climate of relaxation of restrictions on blacks, however unfortunate that prosperity may seem to many Americans. The success of this faith should be taken as only one of the more obvious manifestations of a generally rising level of resentment and militancy among blacks. Thus we can expect to find other groups of unconventional believers similarly moved by a rejection of important elements of the conventional tradition, but in different ways. Thus some black Christians have attempted to channel this feeling into a new version of the Christian faith rather than into something as basically unfamiliar as Islam is to most Americans. Christianity has become a revolutionary faith in a political sense for many people in the contemporary world, for example, for Roman Catholic militants in the conservative societies of Latin America. In a similar way, some black Christians have tried to develop a militant brand of Christianity for blacks.

It is hard to know as yet how significant a movement will result, but one clergyman has achieved a reputation for moving his church in this direction. His name is Albert Cleage, and his church, in Detroit, is called The Shrine of the Black Madonna. As the name implies, this church is founded on the blackness, or at least the non-whiteness, of the mother of Jesus. In his published sermons Cleage has revived an old point of view but given it a new twist. It used to be argued that the epistles of St. Paul in the New Testament were responsible for distorting the original Christian message by the admixture of essentially Greek ideas about salvation and the sinfulness of the flesh. Cleage suggests instead that Paul, in his zeal to transform the Gospel into a message acceptable to Gentiles, in effect accommodated it to the thinking of European people and reduced or destroyed its effectiveness for nonwhites.[8] In this way it can be claimed that only nonwhites, and in America only the minorities who have been subjected to discrimination, can have an authentic sense of what the Gospel means. This is a questionable thesis, but its practical effect may well be to provide an alternative to the rigidity of the Black Muslim organization for black people similarly disenchanted with the traditions of their conventional belief.

Whatever one's point of view regarding the Black Muslims and Cleage's church, the two groups are evidence against the Marxist analysis of how religion works in people's lives. Of course, a sophisticated Marxist analysis might hold that these are simply ways of helping oppressed people raise their consciousness in order to demand and acquire power. Once this has been accomplished, a Marxist might argue, such groups will disappear. If they do survive under changed social conditions, the reason will be that they were more than agencies for social change, that as religious groups they provide people with a transforming vision of human experience.

AN INNOVATIVE EVANGELIST

It is also important to relate that not all unconventional believers among blacks find a new version of their old faith in groups that have rejected what they consider white definitions of reality. There are several black evangelists who work in ways very like those of their white counterparts. One who has developed a very innovative message is Dr. Frederick J. Eikerenkoetter II, "better known as Reverend Ike," as his advertising states. Since he preaches to an almost exclusively black audience—including congregations in New Orleans, New York, and elsewhere—Reverend Ike can be expected to have some of the qualities of the traditional black preacher. And so he does. He is a strong speaker, capable of calling on considerable emotional force. He can sing well, and he knows the Bible well enough to preach his message in the form of exegetical comment on scriptural texts. In other respects, and quite deliberately, he transforms the traditional spirit of Christian, and particularly evangelical, preaching. He steps to the microphone in snappy, even gaudy clothes. With a kind of boyish charm he extols the blessings of mate-

8. See Albert Cleage, *The Black Messiah* (New York: Sheed & Ward, Inc., 1968).

rial well-being—no apostolic poverty for him! In fact, he tells you frankly that "if you want pie in the sky by-and-by when you die, then Reverend Ike is not your man!" He wants you to have that pie right now "with ice cream on top."

In his own way, and to his own unabashed advantage, Reverend Ike is schooling some blacks in something like Norman Vincent Peale's long-familiar "power of positive thinking." Reverend Ike does so, however, with specific reference to the disadvantages of following the old revivalist admonitions to prostrate yourself and feel miserable. Too often, one suspects, this traditional kind of religious psychology has been a way of coming to terms with enforced misery and subordination. By contrast, Reverend Ike's people are on the way up. Their testimonials are given on behalf of progress and success. The traditional emphasis on healing is consistent with this message, and Ike brings forward the asthmatic boy who was healed at a meeting as soon as he arrived in America from the West Indies. But more characteristic is the story of the person who had no money and no job, or was caught in a meaningless situation, and who by demonstrating faith in the power of Reverend Ike's message saw life turned completely around in a matter of days or weeks. The instrumentality of this change is the "blessing plan," by which the believer commits himself to donations to Reverend Ike's United Church. The ancient motive of religious sacrifice—*do ut des*, I give in order that Thou wilt give—has a very personal relevance in this church.

As in other black churches we have described, a high level of showmanship and warmth pervades the services in the church of Reverend Ike.[9] His headquarters in New York City is a grand former movie theater on Upper Broadway, a building somewhat nondescript on the outside but still splendid within with an almost Moorish luxury. The red-carpeted lobby leads to an orchestra and balcony in which every seat is occupied by the time Reverend Ike appears. The stage is carpeted in bright red, and great gold-painted candelabra stand on either side of a red and gold settee. The orchestra pit rises and descends, on occasion lifting into view a pair of young singers or a young man playing drums. At one side of the stage the gilt console of the old theater organ frames the figure of a capable organist. The singing is lively but somewhat more restrained than at Baptist services. The service follows a traditional

9. See various newspaper and periodical articles on "Reverend Ike." There was, for example, an article in *Time* magazine in the issue of December 11, 1972.

order, but the content of the message is a deliberate transformation of many traditional religious themes, performed by an intelligent man through the imaginative use of biblical material.

When Reverend Ike appears, there is a burst of enthusiasm. In his bright clothes he belies the image of the clergyman as a self-effacing man. Ike is their preacher, and he expects to applaud the success of his people and to see them rejoice in his prosperity. He laughs and jokes with the congregation, and the "testifying" he encourages is a series of recitations of how following his leadership paid off in material success and attendant happiness. He encourages people to get acquainted and to adopt the right attitude by standing and shaking the hands of people around them, meanwhile saying to each other "The spirit of God in me blesses the spirit of God in you." It is a nonpolitical message; Ike's advertising states that "people of all races, religions and those with no religion are welcome." More importantly, "the Church is NOT located in Harlem." In his talk to the congregation, the preacher emphasizes that they have no black power among them, only green power, and he tells a story of how in a Southern city he was treated with respect where once he had been turned away—that is to say, he was respected when he returned with money enough to hire a car to drive him. Whatever his intentions about integrating his audience, virtually everyone in his congregation is black. Moreover, most of the people are women.

The Reverend Ike teaches self-confidence and self-reliance, rather than otherworldliness. With a mock show of horror at the boldness of his teaching, he affirms that there is no one up in the sky to hear a prayer, but that the person who prays is really addressing an aspect of himself, and therefore paying heed to, or failing to hear, a message that needs to be heard. Titles on the publications table in the lobby confirm a spiritual kinship, if not a direct historical link, to the movement long known as New Thought, a point of view that similarly translates Christian ideas into an optimistic and self-affirming rather than a self-punitive doctrine and practice.

On the other hand, like many a crasser evangelist Reverend Ike provides his followers with prayer cloths for healing purposes, in return for a suitable contribution. Somehow his charm and intelligence overcome whatever inconsistencies seem to lie between the positive thinking of the one position and the magical ideas of the other. Again the inference is strong that Reverend Ike makes a strong appeal to black people on the way from lower-class to middle-class life styles and attitudes. He tells them that they can abandon without guilt many of the self-defeating ideas that served them when they had to come to terms with a situation of subordination, but which now hold them back. At the same time he gives them a bit of the familiar old religious style, so that they will not feel like strangers in a new world. They follow him with ardent interest.

These examples of unconventional religious groups are sufficient to indicate that even a sophisticated Marxist analysis of them would have difficulty proving that religion works to narcotize minority peoples in general, and black people in particular, at the present time. To ask such a question, in fact, is almost self-defeating, since it assumes that social change is the only thing that matters, and since contrary evidence can be explained as only temporary, not contrary to the thesis. More importantly, these groups indicate that the problems of minority groups in America have a lot to do with how similar their people are in essential respects to the majority population, rather than with how different they seem. The Indian vision that we invoked at the start of this chapter has an archaic beauty, but it does not seem a likely model for the training of even Indian children in days to come. Unconventional believers among blacks, even when openly hostile to white society, nevertheless show that they accept its basic economic values and would form life styles similar to those of whites if they were allowed to.

Black culture has some distinctive and attractive features, but for better or worse, it is not a foreign body any more than is any other ethnic group in America. At least not yet. As we have suggested, the example of the Black Muslims indicates not so much an alternative to pressure for social change as an organized expression of it, as well as a clue to how strong the pressure is. There are many other unconventional religious possibilities for blacks, of course, than the few we have mentioned. There are not many indications that those who adopt such ways would be militant if they did not choose religious directions. Perhaps the true message here is that in America, if you are different in some important way by nature, it helps to be somewhat different also in faith, because faith is the mark of a necessary self-respect.

Unconventional Belief and the Special Need

The power of a particularly compelling message, the quest for a more moving experience of faith, membership in a minority group that asserts, "We matter too, perhaps more than you do"—all these motives have influenced the creation of a great variety of groups of unconventional believers in contemporary America. In the case of racial or ethnic minorities, these groups have a "natural" basis. But it is the particular gift of such groups as the Mormons, as we have seen, to draw together otherwise unrelated people into a group unified by a comprehensive mythology, into a kind of vast extended family or holy nation. Something of the same motive operates in the thinking of Black Muslims, the Nation of Islam. This is not always the basis for organizing groups of unconventional believers, however. Often in the past, especially among people who regarded the Bible as the unquestioned word of God, particular theological ideas provided the basis for drawing individuals out of the everyday social order and shaping them into distinctive groups. Though still possible, a strictly idea-oriented basis of organization is more likely to be replaced nowadays by concern for particular psychological or social needs in the formation of new groups.

One such interest, a perennial one of religious institutions from the beginning of recorded history, is the intense personal concern for success and good health. Much mainline Christian theological interest has focused on the kingdom of God and how it is to be achieved. For Jews the establishment of Israel has been a central concern. But the typical evangelical group has put individual salvation first and dealt with questions of social justice only when forced to, and then generally on the basis of changing enough hearts to make social change inevitable through the concerted efforts of converted individuals. In Protestant liberal denominations, as we shall see later, one manifestation of the unconventional impulse is radical social action in the name of faith. Faith oriented toward social change is perennially impatient with the conservatism of religious institutions; thus people with a religiously motivated social interest may turn to what seem more effective secular means to achieve their ends, ends that seem self-evidently in accord with the will of God. Such people will no longer be counted among unconventional believers, because faith will come to be of only marginal importance for them.

What happens, though, when members of evangelical groups develop an awareness of the need for an unconventional alternative to the decision for Christ? If it no longer seems enough to have a personal relationship with Jesus or to be born again, out of a life of sinfulness and into salvation, how can the idea and the experience of salvation be effectively transformed? One way is to change its basis from an otherworldly to a contemporary reference, so that the goal is not a purer spiritual state of being but a prosperous and successful life. We have seen this kind of motivation at work in the United Church movement led by the black evangelist Reverend Ike. He urges his people to try to be more successful and to cease feeling guilty about it. This kind of doctrinal transformation is typical of several related movements known collectively as New Thought.

On the whole, however, such an emphasis is too foreign to the Christian tradition to be easily reconciled with it except at the cost of considerable criticism, criticism like that which used to be leveled at the Reverend Norman Vincent Peale's doctrine of positive thinking.[1] Much more justifiable, because much more native to the Gospel tradition, is the concern with health and the healing powers of faith. The Reverend Ike touches this base too as part of the demonstration of the virtues of his "blessing plan." But in other groups the stress on healing power is much more direct, and for very understandable reasons. Concern for health is well-nigh universal, and despite the enormous progress of medical science, disease is still a cause of widespread suffering. Disease of any kind is a reminder

1. Peale's most famous work was *The Power of Positive Thinking* (Englewood Cliffs, N.J.: Prentice-Hall, Inc., 1952).

of man's mortality, and where medical treatment is still ineffective, there is a strong tendency to seek supernatural assistance. People who do so can hardly be condemned as escapists when they have no other recourse.

But there is actually a lot of evidence that faith does act as a healing power. The most hardheaded analysis comes from such institutions as the Catholic shrine at Lourdes in the southwestern part of France.[2] Extremely stringent methods are used there to rule out doubtful cures and, as far as possible, all strictly psychological disorders, but at least one person a year is judged to have been cured of serious organic disease after a visit to the shrine. In other words, one need not deny that people have been cured of disease after direct association with a religious place of pilgrimage. It is reasonable to conclude that the pilgrimage to Lourdes has been the instrument of curing many more people than available evidence allows. Many people believe that such a pilgrimage is or may be curative. Their belief and the existence of even a few cures is enough to account for the power of the hope of healing in generating new religious groups.

Perhaps a word or two more may be said about religious healing in general before we look at some of the unconventional groups that have based their teachings on it. The question of the factual credibility of cures by "miraculous" means is the most important question only for those who at all costs want to maintain objectivity and even scepticism about the truth-value of religion. For such people it is important to be shown that people are cured by faith, but for less sceptical people the number of authenticated cures is not the point. In fact it might make very good sense to level criticism at the Catholic Church for being so defensive on this score, so concerned with being intellectually respectable, that it claims far too little on behalf of its healing work. A truly informed knowledge of how healing takes place under any circumstances makes it far more credible that religious healing not only is believed in but actually works. The state of the mind cannot help but affect the body; what are called psychosomatic ailments are the many physical and far from imaginary illnesses from which many people suffer. If faith changes the mental state, many such diseases can be cured. Even the sceptical evangelist Marjoe tells of one such cure of a paralyzed hand that

2. There is a large literature on Lourdes, much of it popular and uncritical. Such works as Louis Rose, *Faith Healing* (Baltimore: Penguin Books, 1968), which evaluates Lourdes and other institutions of religious healing, are probably too sceptical.

took place in his presence and almost convinced him that his work was worthwhile.

Much of the day-to-day practice of medicine involves taking advantage of what is called the "placebo effect"—that is, giving people pills with no active ingredients that "cure" them essentially because of their faith that the doctor knows what the trouble is, and therefore that what he gives as medicine will cure their sickness. Furthermore, the practice of psychiatry and psychotherapy depends on establishing a kind of therapeutic relationship, a relationship of trust that the healer can help the patient to a new outlook, which in many respects is like what a "converted" believer feels.

In the past many such therapeutic functions were performed by special priesthoods, or by men called shamans, who could enter peculiarly intense mental states and exercise healing powers.[3] In our own tradition, when disease was considered a work of demons, a priest could heal by exorcising the evil spirits. Such work is still done, particularly among Spanish-speaking people in American cities, by spiritualists who in many respects perform the functions that middle-class whites expect from mental health professionals. The elaborate rites of exorcism that the spiritualist performs depend on a belief that is threatened by modern education; but in a different kind of way there is a strong component of faith in any quest for health, and people who for any reason are highly preoccupied with health and illness, especially chronic illness, look for religious groups that will attend to these interests. Many evangelical groups stress them, but for some people, health is the primary and perhaps really the only important concern.

THE FAITH HEALER

In the Christian tradition in America, as in many traditions of a quite different sort, faith healing normally means involvement with a personality of extraordinary force. Lourdes is the legacy of Berna-

---

3. For the history of healing and its religious connections, see Walter Addison Jayne, *The Healing Gods of Ancient Civilizations* (New Hyde Park, N. Y.: University Books, 1962); Ari Kiev, *Magic, Faith, and Healing* (New York: The Free Press, 1964); John T. McNeill, *A History of the Cure of Souls* (New York: Harper and Row, Publishers, Inc., 1951); and, for the implications of psychotherapy, Jerome Frank, *Persuasion and Healing* (New York: Schocken Books, Inc., 1963), a new edition of which was published by the Johns Hopkins Press in the spring of 1973.

dette Soubirous and of her visions of the Virgin Mary a little more than a century ago. For us such power is much less closely associated with particular places and much more so with people who project a sense of holy well-being, who communicate the confidence that we too can somehow become free of pain. It is hardly surprising, this being the case, that healers, like the successful evangelists, have made abundant use of modern media in their work. Oral Roberts and Kathryn Kuhlman are perhaps more familiar on television than other healers. Roberts, like the Reverend Ike, emphasizes what you need to do to help yourself into a healthy frame of mind, to cooperate with what God wants to do to heal you. In recent years Roberts has turned to a concern for education, giving prominent roles to his son and daughter-in-law in the use of music on his broadcasts and inculcating Christian values there and in the university founded in Tulsa and named after him. Many people, however, think of him as first and foremost a healer.

Kathryn Kuhlman also relates her work of healing to a traditional evangelistic style. From a base in Denver she has moved out to regular meetings in various locations in the Los Angeles area, with large crowds in attendance. Doubtless her television programs have brought her preaching to more people than have seen her in person, but the dominant theme of all her appearances is an attitude of caring. The evangelical theology exemplified in her work has a number of interesting themes, derived in part from the old Methodist concern for perfection or sanctification as a possibility for those who have experienced salvation in this life. The modern outcome of this theological position is a doctrine encountered fairly often among groups of unconventional believers who base their practice on New Testament principles. It is the belief that the blessings promised in the Scriptures to those who have faith in Christ can somehow be "claimed." This is in some ways a daring extension of the idea of sanctification, which refers primarily to the holy way of living demonstrated by those who have been favored by the grace of God. One acts in a holy way because of what one has received, but that one should be able to claim further benefits from God is to assume a kind of initiative for himself that much Christian thinking would disavow. Naturally, therefore, one does not do so lightly. Miss Kuhlman has written movingly of the deep personal experience she had when her father died, and she realized in looking at his body that what counted about him was really alive and available to her. Her dead father, she writes, "knows that now I constantly lay my head on the shoulder of the Heavenly Father, knowing I can claim

all the blessings of Heaven through Jesus Christ." [4] Good health
has become the blessing that many people have felt her preaching
allowed them to claim.

The widespread visibility of such individuals as Oral Roberts and
Kathryn Kuhlman through television obviously establishes the high
degree of interest in religious healing even in the most technologi-
cally sophisticated society in the world. And we have suggested that
no degree of progress in medical science is likely to eradicate this
interest entirely. But by the same token we would like to see
whether something more positive can be said, whether we can find
groups whose beliefs are based on concern for health as a primary
religious goal and sustained by the belief that health can be
achieved through the common participation in the rituals of a
church. The example that comes immediately to mind is Christian
Science, a group whose origins are now more than a century behind
us but one that nevertheless remains a religious institution with a
certain amount of evangelical zeal. A better example, perhaps—
since Christian Science is so established as not to qualify on first
examination as an unconventional group—is a group of much more
recent origin, probably more dynamic though in many ways related
to the ways of Christian Science, and above all much more accepting
of the implications of modern technology. This is the Church of
Scientology.

HEALING GROUPS

These two groups are interesting for both their similarities and their
differences. In the first place, like other groups devoted to religious
healing, these base their appeal on extraordinary personalities—
Christian Science on Mary Baker Eddy and Scientology on L. Ron
Hubbard. Both have developed theories that depend on the cultivation of ever higher levels of spiritual reality and regard such attainment as the fruit of attention to correct religious principles and dis-
ciplines. In practice their organizations depend on networks of
trained practitioners who communicate the teachings of the founders to others as the basis for what the groups consider effective
therapy for a wide variety of ailments. Both groups have become
churches in the sense of creating liturgies for services of worship,

4. This story was originally printed in *Guideposts* and is quoted from *Logos
Journal* 39, 9 (September–October 1971), 5.

thereby placing themselves among the established denominations. In this role they declare their kinship to the Christian tradition but also depart significantly from the ways in which that tradition has normally been interpreted. For them the concern for health is central.

The major differences between the two groups will appear in our comparison of them. One difference is, of course, a consequence of the fact that Christian Science is much older and expresses the characteristic interests of the latter half of the nineteenth rather than the twentieth century. Is that to say that the two groups are in a way equivalent, except that they are products of their times? There is something to be said for such a point of view, but the fact remains that Christian Science is also a living institution today, perhaps competing with Scientology for some of the same people's allegiance. It is important, therefore, to see how they appear in their contemporary dress alongside each other.

Let us go therefore to meetings of both groups, as we have done before, and build from these impressions some sense of each group's reality. Christian Science, as we have already indicated, owes much to nineteenth-century Protestant forms. One significant point in its identity, however, is a centralized structure for which only perhaps the Mormon Church provides a good comparison, and then only in some respects. All Christian Science churches are branches of what is called the Mother Church, located in Boston and bearing to outlying churches of Christ, Scientist, much the same relation as Mary Baker Eddy, the founder of the movement, bore to the developing church in her day. Her presence is emphasized again and again in what is spoken and read. Since the doctrine of Christian Science asserts that the only true reality is spiritual, she remains the fountainhead of the religious impulse of all the Christian Science churches. A symbol of her importance is the fact that her words are put on a level equal to those of the Bible. In one church the great arch over the chancel carries these words: "God is Love and He that Dwelleth in Love Dwelleth in God and God in Him." This is scriptural, being a quotation from one of the epistles of John. On the walls on either side, however, are quotations from Mary Baker Eddy on the one hand, and Jesus Christ on the other. On the left, from Mrs. Eddy, comes the message that "Divine Love always has met and always will meet every human need." On the right, from Jesus Christ, there is a motto also carried in Christian Science literature: "The kingdom of heaven is at hand. Heal the sick. Cleanse the lepers. Raise the Dead. Cast out Devils." Hymns in the hymn book are set to Mrs. Eddy's words, as is even the music sung by the soloist.

The theme of the coordinate authority of Mary Baker Eddy and Christ is most conspicuous, perhaps, in the major feature of the service, the so-called "lesson-sermon." Christian Science has no formal clergy. The affairs of the Mother Church, and therefore to some degree those of all the branch churches, are directed by a central staff, and the structure of the organization is based on a widespread network of "practitioners," people trained to assist others in the use of texts and traditions for healing and general spiritual advancement. In the services, however, people elected periodically as First and Second Reader cooperate in leading worship, and there is therefore nothing like the sermon familiar to most Protestant churchgoers. On this occasion the two readers alternated in delivering passages prescribed in a pamphlet of Bible lessons. One read from the Bible, the other from *Science and Health,* written by Mrs. Eddy and expounding her metaphysical religious philosophy. In this symbolic way it is demonstrated that for Christian Science the two books have equal status.

It is also noteworthy that of the two readers at this service, one is a man and the other a woman, and that though the ushers who collect the offering are men, women stand at the head of each aisle during those portions of the service when the people join in singing or prayer. Mrs. Eddy in fact echoes a theme that before her time appeared in the teachings of only a few sectarian groups—the theme that the feminine deserves equal rank with the masculine. Mother Ann Lee, founder of the Shakers in the eighteenth century, asserted that she herself was the "female principle in Christ," and that therefore the second coming was fulfilled in the group she led.[5] The Shakers were still a noteworthy group in Mrs. Eddy's time, and other groups like the Oneida community had sexual equality as a major point of doctrine and practice.[6] Mrs. Eddy in some ways anticipates Jung in writing that "union of the masculine and feminine qualities constitutes completeness." The difference between her and Jung is that from the point of view of depth psychology her thinking works primarily on the level of consciousness and takes account of what would be called unconscious or instinctual forces only in terms of what she calls "animal magnetism." This is a force representing not only what is worst in the human constitution, but something that can be denied because strictly speaking it does not exist. Otherwise

5. For more information on the Shakers, see Edward Andrews, *The People Called Shakers* (New York: Dover Publications, Inc., 1963).

6. There are brief discussions of the Oneida Community and many similar groups in Bryan Wilson, *Religious Sects* (New York: McGraw-Hill Book Company, 1970).

it needs to be fended off when used in a hostile way by outsiders against herself and against the movement she founded.

This is not the place to go into detail about the doctrine of Christian Science. Suffice it to say that what is meant by the word "science" in the name of the Christian Science Church is a systematic mental self-discipline whose aim is the demonstration to oneself that "Mind is All." Pain, illness, and in general any disharmony are revealed under careful analysis as in fact only a perception, and therefore as a mental event that has no reality apart from its effects and can be dealt with on the mental level. The body is, in effect, only a vehicle for the mind, and one schools oneself to assert the primacy of mind over gross matter by reading *Science and Health,* other authorized literature, and the Bible as interpreted by the church. Should any illness strike despite this discipline, it is dealt with by discussions with one of the several practitioners available in every region where Christian Science maintains itself.

Christian Science teaches, therefore, that health is the aim of a spiritual quest. This is not to say that health is the only concern of the faith, but its importance is shown by its primary role in the testimonies that replace the Sunday lesson sermon in the Wednesday evening meetings. Conventional medicine is largely rejected because of its preoccupation with "material remedies." [7] This does not mean, however, that Christian Scientists reject all medical therapy. The church maintains sanatoria and publishes a directory of nurses who will perform "the practical duties necessary in the care of the sick but who give no medication or any physical application beyond the normal measures of cleanliness." Normally Christian Science practitioners cannot be called in on a case if a physician is attending, but the church specifies some exceptions to this rule—childbirth, when law requires the presence of a physician or midwife, and so-called mechanical ailments, such as broken bones, which may be set by a physician if the believer does not wish to rely on the faith alone. The critical factor is the use of medication, which is avoided because of the fundamental belief in the unreality of matter and the corollary error that would be involved in reliance on material remedies.

It may be difficult to see in Christian Science a good example of unconventional belief in the same sense as our previous examples. Its churches are thoroughly conventional in design—not much different from Methodist structures in the arrangement of lectern and

7. Such information is given in official pamphlets available at Christian Science churches and reading rooms.

organ, and, in the reliance on testimonies of believers, formally not too far from the practice of evangelical faiths generally. It is obvious, moreover, that the faith appeals most to a settled middle-class constituency and avoids emotional enthusiasm. Family people and particularly women of mature years find its teachings very congenial, its methods appropriate to their emotional as well as physical needs. In its origins it was a controversial and certainly unconventional pattern of belief, and the Mother Church and its branches remain the object of much curiosity to outsiders, but like many similar groups, it finds itself hard-pressed to maintain its original zeal.

On the other hand, perhaps this is not the way to put it, because it may be that many, even most of the adherents of Christian Science do not want their church to be seen as something exotic or strange. It is said, for example, that the original edition of Mrs. Eddy's *Science and Health* has been considerably modified in later versions to blunt the sharp edges of some of her more extreme statements. The Mother Church, not wanting to seem an institution of the middle-aged, has sponsored impressive rallies in recent years for young people, and it has filmed at least one such event to show that its message is still lively; but even this was obviously in respectable contrast to the rock music and drugs of young people who were called the "Woodstock generation," so that it is hard not to conclude that Christian Science has become a conventional institution, hardly distinguishable in most respects from the conventional churches.

THE CHURCH OF SCIENTOLOGY

The deep concern for health has not lost its power to generate groups of unconventional believers, however, as can be recognized from the dynamism and rapid growth of another, though a more recent, group founded on many of the same premises as Christian Science. The comparison with this new group, the Church of Scientology, is remarkably interesting. Scientology owes its existence to a man named L. (for Lafayette) Ron Hubbard, who has managed to impress his way of thinking on a considerable number of followers. Like Christian Science, Scientology proclaims itself a gospel appropriate to the modern age—the age of science and technology—for the realization of age-old spiritual benefits. Like Christian Science, Scientology proclaims itself a therapy for many ills. Under the stress of encounters with governmental agencies, it has moderated some of its earlier claims, but it offers a therapeutic approach at least to psychological difficulties, an approach that puts it at odds with established medical practice.

Scientology recently has adapted its techniques to the problems of narcotics addicts, thereby inviting comparison with the religious aspects of such programs as that of Alcoholics Anonymous and related groups. In addition, like Christian Science and many other dynamic modern groups, Scientology prospers in large measure by means of the publication of large quantities of literature, especially books and pamphlets by Mr. Hubbard. While Christian Science publishes a conservative and highly respected newspaper of national scope, the daily *Christian Science Monitor,* and a variety of weekly, monthly, and quarterly publications such as books, magazines, and pamphlets, Scientology offers a wide assortment of books in which Hubbard relates its principles to many social, medical, and spiritual problems. Finally, the distinctiveness of Scientology's beliefs and practices, and the abundant self-confidence of Hubbard in promoting them as therapeutic, have created a highly organized international movement that many people credit with responsibility for transforming and perfecting their lives.

A significant means of comparison of the two groups is the study of the single book that is of central importance to each movement. Whereas it was *Science and Health* in the case of Christian Science, in the background of Scientology is a book by Hubbard entitled *Dianetics: The Modern Science of Mental Health.*[8] Originally published in 1950, the book became a best-seller, capitalizing on the widespread interest in psychoanalytic and psychological approaches. In the years between Mary Baker Eddy and Hubbard, the advance of medical science had made it more difficult to gain wide credibility for a general theory of "mind over matter" in the treatment of diseases. On the other hand, psychoanalytic theory had been based on the assumption that many organic ailments were determined by purely psychological factors and could be cured by talking about one's state of mind with a professional psychiatrist. The first psychoanalytic cases were cases of this kind, and out of such concerns developed the field of psychosomatic medicine. This field did not include diseases caused by identifiable microbes or viruses or other agents external to the body, but it certainly was possible to speculate that the course of any illness might be affected by psychosomatic factors, and thus possibly that a sufferer's difficulty might be alleviated if not altogether eradicated by mental discipline.

In a way, therefore, Scientology was from its beginning a kind

8. L. Ron Hubbard, *Dianetics* (New York: Paperback Library, 1968).

of Western yoga, just as Christian Science was. The difference is that the reference point for the newer faith is not medical science in general but the treatment of mental illness in particular. *Dianetics* was not at all modest in its claims. Recognizing the validity of the "germ theory of disease," dianetics marks off as its own area the complementary "nongerm theory of disease," and the book states that "the problem of psychosomatic illness is entirely embraced by dianetics, and by dianetic technique such illness has been eradicated entirely in every case.[9] Hubbard even speculates on the possibility that his therapy may be useful against cancer and diabetes, although he takes pains to deny any claims to provide cures for these diseases. He speculates about what predisposes people to illness, and he suggests that dianetics provides a way to decrease or eliminate that predisposition. Dianetics allegedly does so by eliminating "engrams" —traces of perceptions received by an individual during a period of unconsciousness, especially at those times during which the individual experienced physical or emotional pain in the past.

In dianetics and in the techniques of Scientology derived from dianetics, engrams are considered dangerous because they are not memories and are therefore not accessible to conscious thought. Being uncontrollable, they leave their mark on bodily processes— hence causing psychosomatic illness—and retain a tremendous power to work damage to psychic health, and particularly to interfere with "the single and sole purpose"—survival. This is because the mind is divided into two entities, the "analytical" and the "reactive" mind banks (the language of modern technology has had an important place in the formulation of the theory). The analytical mind is conscious, and it stores up memories; the reactive mind, by contrast, stores engrams, and engrams are pain traces of one sort or another.[10] This theory is better, I suspect, than the Christian Science idea that pain is only an illusion, but we must ask the question whether engrams—whatever they correspond to in other versions of the human personality—can be dealt with effectively in this way.

SCIENTOLOGY IN PRACTICE

Here we may enter the practice of Scientology as someone might who had been intrigued by the text of a poster, enticed by the invitation to a free meeting, or impressed by a friend who had once been

9. *Ibid.*, p. 106.
10. *Ibid.*, Book II, Chapters 1 and 2.

confused but now seemed more sure of himself. Here is where the technology comes in. Scientology does not leave the removal of engrams to a process of reading and meditation or to mere discussion with a practitioner. Instead it relies on a process called "auditing." [11] The trained practitioner is called an "auditor," and the new trainee, the "preclear," agrees to submit to the auditor's detailed questioning about his inner life. Essential to this process is the use of a device called the "E-meter," or electropsychometer, which passes a low electrical current through the skin of subjects being questioned. In a manner similar to that of a lie detector machine, the E-meter registers a visible change when the subject has an emotional response to a question. At such points in the questioning, the auditor encourages the preclear to try to get at the source of the emotional response. Becoming what is called a "clear" involves long discipline in auditing, until any past experience that left engrams can be transformed into a memory, its negative emotional energy discharged.

In a way this process resembles deep psychoanalysis, and part of the popularity of the book *Dianetics* seems to have come from the hope that the results of psychoanalysis could be obtained in a shorter time, and at much less expense, by the process of auditing. Not least of all, the work could be done by laymen trained only by undergoing the process themselves. Since the early 1950s, Hubbard has propagated the method successfully, despite some false starts and a number of setbacks that might have defeated a less formidable man. Some early medical interest in his ideas and procedures was followed by scepticism when his results turned out to be less than his claims, and so the movement changed direction.[12] "Dianetic research institutes" set up in the early 1950s seemed on the point of failure, and so in 1952 the movement was reborn as Scientology. Scientology is now presented as a mental discipline capable of taking people through a number of levels of personality development in ways suggesting some of the concepts of an Eastern religion like Hinduism, or those of some esoteric Western groups.

Granted this new direction of Hubbard's thinking, it is not altogether surprising that he seemed to turn from science, and the attempt to demonstrate a wonder-working cure, to the attempt to establish the credentials of Scientology as a religion. In 1955 a Founding Church of Scientology was established in Washington, D.C., and another in New York City. A relic of old ideological

11. *Ibid.*, Book III, Chapter 3. See also more recent Scientology literature.
12. George Malko, *Scientology* (New York: Delacorte Press, 1970). A mimeographed refutation of Malko was given me by Priscilla Hailes, minister of public information of the New York Church of Scientology.

warfare, perhaps, was a raid by the Food and Drug Administration
in 1963 on the Washington church, on the ground that the claims
made for the E-meter were fraudulent. In subsequent years the
organization ran into similar difficulties in England and Australia.
But in 1971 a district judge in Washington, D.C., ruled that in
order to justify the seizure of E-meters and Scientology literature,
the government agency would have to prove that Scientology was
not a religion. Failing that, the confiscated materials would have to
be returned and practitioners of Scientology left to pursue their
interests unmolested.[13] There were conditions, to be sure. Only those
who qualified as clergy by the definition of the Church of Scientology
could use the E-meter as an adjunct to their pastoral work, and no
healing claims could be made for its use. Meters and literature distributed by the various churches of the movement now bear printed
or stamped disclaimers of intent to cure.

Is such a movement really a religion, or does it only pretend
to be in order to find safety in the separation of church and state in
America? More importantly, can it maintain itself despite a history
of controversy, seemingly questionable practices, and innuendoes
about its financial structure? Why do people go on supporting it?
The answer to the last question has to be that people support it
because they think they are getting something worthwhile out of it,
and because of this feeling they are able to overlook attacks and
criticisms because as insiders they "know better." That is, within
the organization its integrity is defended, and since people remain
because they feel helped by Scientology, the movement cannot be
evil from their point of view. As a matter of fact, even if the worst
that could be said about L. Ron Hubbard were proved true, that
would not necessarily make a fundamental difference, so long as the
movement remained valuable to enough people. Scientology would
not be the first religious group founded by someone of less than the
highest spiritual credentials, and certainly the history of religious
healing is studded with examples of countless sufferers hoping
against hope, fanatically devoted to the mere possibility of getting
better through faith. Medical science has done wonders for us, but
it cannot do everything, and above all it cannot cure us of what
some have called the ultimate disease, mortality. Thus healing faiths
can be expected to retain their power.

How does Scientology measure up against such a backdrop? Sur-
prisingly well, considering many of the groups it could be compared

13. See "The Findings on the U. S. Food and Drug Agency," published in
1968 by The Department of Publications World Wide (a Scientology publishing
organization).

with. Much of its literature could be said to be militantly defensive, but countless controversial religious movements have taken on such a posture in their early days. The reputation for fanaticism may be a response to the distinctive personality of the founder, who asserts a new point of view against the almost inevitable opposition of established interests. In this respect Hubbard is little different from Mary Baker Eddy, Joseph Smith, or even John Wesley. All were argumentative and had to be, or become, single-minded in defense of their position. Even so antireligious a man as Sigmund Freud displayed the same characteristics in his defense of psycho-analysis, which to this day many medical scientists consider more of a mythology than a science.[14] If you visit a Scientology center in one of the major cities where the movement is well established, you find it a bustling place, filled mostly with people neither crippled, ugly nor sick in any obvious way. By contrast to Christian Science, Scien-tology has made peace with medicine, and as an indicator of its good faith asserts that it requires new preclears to undergo physical examinations by licensed physicians before they begin their auditing discipline.

In other words, the practice of Scientology parallels that of psy-chotherapy in many respects. It is understandable that the medical authorities who have responsibility for mental health programs should look upon it with disfavor as poorly controlled and overly mystical, in the same way they view Christian Science. But by the same token, the claims of Scientology to be a religion have to be evaluated fairly, and on this score the evidence is mixed. It is appar-ent, on the one hand, that the church makes no very great invest-ment of effort in corporate worship. In fact, the book of "back-ground and ceremonies" it publishes begins with the distinction be-tween religious philosophies and religious practices, to the detri-ment of particular practices.[15] Ordinary services are really informal lectures, deliberately undogmatic in content; they are therefore ex-tensions of the point of view established in the literature and in the auditing practice. The service book makes contact with many tradi-tions by quoting the wisdom of the ages, but its only claim on behalf of Scientology is for total freedom from authoritarian restraints in the pursuit of man's highest nature. There are ceremonial forms for marriage, "naming" (as opposed to baptism or christening), and

14. See for example Freud's "On the History of the Psycho-Analytic Move-ment," published in 1914 and reprinted in volume I of his *Collected Papers* (New York: Basic Books, Inc., 1959).

15. See *The Background and Ceremonies of the Church of Scientology of California, World Wide,* published in 1970.

funerals, but it does not appear that the minister must follow the printed form. Even the rather optimistic Creed of the Church of Scientology is not something to be recited in a formally prescribed way.

On the other hand, there are in the teaching some recognizably religious ideas—not very original ones, to be sure, but perhaps therefore all the more effective. One example may give an impression of what they are. In the service book it is said that "the main purpose of a Naming Ceremony is to help get the thetan oriented." Further, "he has recently taken over the new body." What is this "thetan"? One statement in Scientology literature declares "that man is a spiritual being, not a body, not a mind, but a nonphysical, spiritual entity who uses a mind and body to play the games of existence in the physical universe," and that the thetan (from the Greek letter *theta*) is this entity.[16]

This belief in a preexistent spiritual entity as the true human reality is not far from the premises of Christian Science and of some other religious philosophies of the West and the East. It seems to be the chief point of difference between Scientology and the belief system proposed in *Dianetics,* which puts much stress on prenatal influences on the fundamental cellular structure of human existence but stops short of making a spiritual entity primary. One result of the use of the doctrine of a thetan in the practice of Scientology is that to become a "clear" through auditing discipline is not the final stage of spiritual growth. At higher levels the thetan can become liberated from gross involvement in matter, energy, space, and time (the acronym MEST in the lexicon of Scientology, which puts a premium on easy and contemporary-sounding modes of communication). This is a religious point of view, and it must be admitted that Scientology provides a kind of technological yoga for realizing it.

It is expensive to reach these levels in Scientology, as many of its critics have been delighted to point out. But such criticism really misses the mark, because so long as people feel that the benefits are worth the cost of the auditing courses and want *their* thetans to climb to the highest levels of spirituality, they are willing to pay. There is little or no evidence that they are forced to pay against their will. In fairness it must be pointed out that a satisfactory course of psychotherapy is also expensive, and that it is no novelty to find considerable sums of money contributed to what people believe is their spiritual enrichment. In summary, it is too early to render any

16. The source of this statement is the mimeographed refutation of Malko (see above, footnote 12).

final verdict on whether Scientology will maintain itself as a vital religion. Since Christian Science succeeded in maintaining itself despite its greater distance from the canons of medical science, there is reason to believe that Scientology also will realize as an organized movement what it proposes to individuals as the highest human goal, Survival with a capital 'S.' It may do so if sufficient numbers of people continue to believe that in thinking as they think, and practicing as they practice together, they constitute a genuine community of faith.

This is, after all, the only true test of the validity of any religious group. It is obvious that the quest for health is one of several broad preoccupations that are so compelling and so transcendent of the limits of rational planning as to be persistently the basis for religious groups in the foreseeable future. It is easy to foresee that the desperately ill will continue to follow the charismatic figures who claim to be able to bring them relief. But the power of Scientology to move those who are young and healthy shows how much more is at stake in matters of health than simply the well-being of the body.

Church,
Denomination, and the
Unconventional Believer

GIVE ME ALSO THIS POWER

Many, many more examples could be given of innovative and dynamic religious groups that have prospered in the recent past in America. As was indicated at the start, however, the reasons for the amount of attention they have drawn may give the wrong impression about the religious life of the country, particularly about where the most active religious life is. We have examined several unconventional groups that seem especially vigorous and have caught the public eye for a variety of reasons, but others could be singled out as cases of decline. To be new is not necessarily to be prosperous.

In addition, several general considerations have entered into a kind of unspoken agreement among writers that only the unconventional groups are really alive and therefore merit serious attention. Some of the reasons for this consensus are clear enough. Recent years have been a time of unusually rapid social change in which groups previously subordinate and discriminated against have asserted themselves and made open claims for dignity and status equal to that of other groups in our society. It has become possible for a clergyman from the Church of God of Prophecy, one of the more conservative religious groups in America, to come out as a declared homosexual and to found a church for homosexuals. It is hardly surprising that this event was newsworthy, more so than the founding of any number of conventional congregations. It is also hardly surprising that the clergyman lost his credentials with his parent church. It has been a time when conventional institutions have tended to be very much on the defensive or in open disarray, a time when the so-called counter-culture has developed religious directions that have seemed to hold the promise of being the true paths to the future.[1]

But is this appearance also the reality? Is all the growth and religious vitality confined to the edges of the historic institutions, to the

1. See Winthrop S. Hudson, *Religion in America,* 2d ed. (New York: Charles Scribner's Sons, 1973), the new final chapter.

conservative and fundamentalist groups on the one hand and to the radical ones on the other? A lot of the available evidence suggests so, but it needs to be interpreted with care. Perhaps the most misleading aspect of the situation is how much conventional religious bodies have contributed to the impression of their own decline. True, one hard bit of evidence is the decline in church attendance, and that must be taken seriously. Yet other facts are not so clear. A centralized organization like the National Council of Churches, located in New York City, has suffered a drastic loss of financial support, but there is considerable evidence that a kind of backlash against its more radical efforts on behalf of social change is part of the reason. More important than this, other evidence suggests that money given for support of church projects is being retained and used at the local level, rather than sent on for global projects.[2]

Furthermore, the intellectual traditions and the training institutions for clergy in the mainline denominations have run into a loss of purpose and morale that seems in many ways more serious than what is happening out in the local churches. It is curious that when the churches were most prosperous, during the fifties and early sixties, the theological ideas that drew the most attention, at least in the seminaries of liberal Protestantism, provided a basis for severe criticism of conventional religion. There was great enthusiasm for efforts at a high level to dissolve barriers among denominations and to involve the churches at all levels in constructive social change. General disillusionment with the results of these programs is a major theme of the years when the war in Southeast Asia replaced domestic concerns as the main focus for social activism. At the same time religious thinkers became interested in such topics as the theology of the "death of God," or what was called "religionless Christianity." Both of these topics were directed toward showing that conventional ways of thinking about God and worshiping in churches were passé.[3]

In some ways such ideas continued the earlier trends of thought, but they may also be the theological counterpart of the process of disillusionment. More recently, the "theology of hope" had a little more to offer to traditions of a more conventional kind, but there has also been a lot of "theology of revolution," not just on behalf of blacks and other minority groups, but in support of rapid and even

2. For the decline in National Council finances, see articles published in 1970 in the journal *Christianity Today*.

3. See John MacQuarrie, *Contemporary Religious Thinkers* (New York: Harper and Row, Publishers, Inc., 1968).

violent social change in many parts of the world.[4] Such thinking has naturally not evoked much ardent support in the churches, with the result that some have seen a widening gap between clergy and the people to whom they minister. One response in conservative churches has been reinforcement of more traditional forms of faith, as we have seen. In the days of "death of God" thinking, for example, in the so-called Bible Belt, many an automobile could be seen carrying a bumper sticker with the legend, "Our God is not dead. Sorry about yours."

NEW WINE IN OLD BOTTLES

All these examples of negative evidence, and many more that could be cited, argue that the older forms of faith are entirely conventional, that they have lost any capacity to offer really vital experience to the unconventional believer. Is this true? In answer, perhaps it is appropriate, since much of what we have in mind is the Christian tradition, to examine some biblical examples in an effort to see whether such a conclusion is misleading. Jesus, one may discover, presented his teaching as a novel message, a new wine that ought not be poured into old bottles, presumably for fear of contamination or spoilage. This would suggest that all authenticity must lie with new forms of the faith—thus with groups of unconventional believers. But such an image may be deceptive, especially in our time. For there is very little that is new in any presentation of the ancient faith, and many new groups present themselves as reformers, restorers of the truth of the past. And the age-old image of old bottles no longer holds for us since bottles can be cleaned, reused, and even recycled.

It may be more useful, therefore, to look for an alternative image with different implications. The title of this introduction is intended to present such an image. It comes from a story in the New Testament book of the Acts of the Apostles. Simon Magus, a famous magician and wonder worker with a large following, is shown in the

4. On recent theological developments, see the series of volumes entitled *New Theology*, edited by Martin Marty and Dean Peerman and published by Macmillan, Inc. Volumes 6, 8, and 9 are concerned with various revolutionary themes. For a black perspective, see James H. Cone, *Black Theology and Black Power* (New York: The Seabury Press, 1969). For information on the clergy-laity gap, see Jeffrey K. Hadden, *The Gathering Storm in the Churches* (Garden City, N.Y.: Doubleday and Company, Inc., 1969).

eighth chapter of the book as so impressed by the wonders he sees the apostles performing that he wants to have the same power himself. The power in question is the power of the Holy Spirit, that height of exaltation that is the focus of all pentecostal seeking, now as then. Simon asks for the power but is indignantly refused. The reason is not that he is a magician, for it is clear from the story that Simon respects the apostles' power more than his own. It is rather that he fails to understand its inner intention, so much so that he tries to buy the power with money, to add it to his bag of tricks, so to speak. The outsider sees the power of faith, and he envies it. It is not wrong to want it, unless you want it as a means of enhancing your reputation.

Thus the conventional believers, and the churches they belong to, may be seen as standing a bit uncomfortably in something like Simon's position. They see more power elsewhere, in the groups of unconventional believers, and they are not wrong to desire more of it for themselves. But there is no reason why they can't have it, so long as they understand what it is really all about. The problem is that, like Simon, they may be diverted by the wrong reasons, the most common of which is the need to keep their institutions going, to raise budgets, keep buildings in repair, recruit new members, and manage prudently. As we have seen previously, this is not necessarily bad—not even bad religion—despite the ready criticism of it. This kind of religion, however, is not lively, not exciting, and not therefore the religion that will attract or satisfy the unconventional believer.

It is at this point that biblical illustrations may reveal their limitations, because churches are groups of people, and many things can happen within them. To return to the argument of the start of the book, it must be recognized that the unconventional religious impulse can arise anywhere. One must expect to find it present in any religious group, in certain individuals. So the question is, what happens to it? Does it find adequate expression? Is it suppressed, or is it possible that unconventional believers, when in the midst of conventional groups, tend to be lost sight of only because they are in the midst of the greater number of conventional believers? It may be, in fact, that the unconventional believers in conventional groups may be more numerous, and even more interesting, than those who seem more lively just because they are more conspicuous in smaller groups.

This line of argument, it should be emphasized, is more a hypothesis than a conclusion, a case intended to prepare the reader to look at some facts not usually presented when unconventional religious groups are described or analyzed. What follows is evidence that will leave the final decision up to the reader, or perhaps stimulate a search for more evidence. Examples of unconventional religious expression do present themselves in conventional groups, and the three chapters following organize them according to the three conventional divisions of American religion. First we look at the Roman Catholic Church, once among the most rigidly controlled of all the traditions represented here, then Judaism, and finally the Protestant denominations. When we have done so, we may have the basis for a sound judgment about the religious value of different kinds of groups.

Unconventional Believers
and Catholic Renewal

It is hardly an exaggeration to say that nothing has been the same for Roman Catholics since a day early in 1959 when Pope John XXIII, a rotund and kindly old Italian churchman, announced his intention to convoke a council of the Church. This was to be an ecumenical council in a tradition going back to the fourth century. The word "ecumenical" is a technical term signifying that the entire church is represented and that therefore the council is a gathering of all in one house, symbolically speaking. But this council, the Second Vatican Council, or Vatican II, was noteworthy in more than just a historical sense. Its ecumenical character extended beyond the traditional Catholic concerns, which would have been expressed in the inclusion only of those who could be considered legitimately Catholic in doctrine and in willingness to acknowledge the authority of Rome. But in this case Pope John made sincere gestures of friendship and good will to Protestants, whom Catholics had in recent years begun to call "separated brethren," and to the Eastern Orthodox churches, whose history is as rich and ancient as that of the Roman Catholic Church but whose government had been linked to that of the Eastern Roman Empire and had been wholly separated from the Western Church for more than nine centuries. An era of mutual charity was being inaugurated.[1]

1. For a chronicle of the council, see "Xavier Rhynne," *Vatican Council II* (New York: Farrar, Straus and Giroux, Inc., 1968).

Of course, it is significant that a single man's decision could make such a difference. Non-Catholics have often had extravagant ideas of the degree of power that could be wielded over Catholics by the Vatican. Until the election of President John F. Kennedy in 1960, many Americans felt that Rome dictated the political behavior of their Catholic countrymen. But it is true that a trend toward greater papal authority had existed for several centuries and had been confirmed most strongly in the nineteenth-century reaction to the democratic excesses of the French Revolution. Thus in response to European political conditions, as well as to long-established internal developments in the image that members of the Church held of it, the Roman Catholic community granted the pope, whose name means "father," an authority few natural fathers could aspire to.

It is important to qualify such statements, because in areas where the Church was not dominant, it was troubled by the stirrings of other ideas of authority. These were dealt with by the resolute application of paternal discipline—by admonition and in some cases excommunication. At the turn of the century, for example, a kind of thinking labeled "modernism," which shared much with the thinking coming to the fore in the major Protestant denominations in this country, was condemned as heretical and its leading thinkers disgraced. In 1899 a letter from Pope Leo XIII to the American Church condemned what he called "Americanism," the idea that Catholics should emphasize what they had in common with Protestants and other religious groups, and the idea that the Catholic Church here should be different from the Church elsewhere. Insofar as they had the power to do so, those who had authority in the Church opposed most of the central trends of modern civilization.[2]

In retrospect it is easy to see that a change was inevitable so long as these trends persisted. In most European countries, especially since World War I and World War II, the forms of political authority had become increasingly democratic; even totalitarian governments instituted the form, if not the substance, of popular control of institutions. The Church was left looking like the "divine right" monarchy that had been replaced everywhere. Where thought was the issue, the triumphs of science continued to undermine confidence in a system based on a prescientific revelation, proclaimed by an institutional hierarchy that allowed no fundamental questions to be asked. Not least of all, the images of family relations, which were so important to the ways in which the faith and worship of Roman

2. See H. Shelton Smith, Robert T. Handy, and Lefferts A. Loetscher, eds., *American Christianity* (New York: Charles Scribner's Sons, 1960), Vol. 2 for documents on Modernism and Americanism.

Catholicism were expressed, and the morality constructed on those images (including prohibition of divorce and artificial means of birth control) had come to be no longer taken for granted by many people. How many fathers now crave the absolute obedience of their children? For how many people today, even among the Catholic priesthood, does chastity seem self-evidently a mark of the holy life? Even in Italy, after long and bitter controversy, divorce has been legalized.

Thus the initiative of Pope John XXIII in calling the first ecumenical council held in almost a century has to be seen as a reversal of the nineteenth-century direction. Many Catholic leaders felt that if the Church wished to remain widely influential, it had to become more in touch with the ways most of its people were moving in response to the cultural developments of their civilization. America could now be seen as an example of the possibility of success of the Catholic Church in a free, competitive, and very modern environment. The warmth of the response to Pope John, it seems fair to say, was not one of awe in the face of his power, but was one of gratitude that he allowed freer expression of energies latent in the experience of many contemporary Catholics. This is why things cannot ever be the same again in the Roman Catholic Church. The decision to convoke Vatican II may well be the last papal decision of such critical importance, for in its aftermath even the doctrine of papal infallibility, which in many ways was the touchstone of the former ideas of Catholic authority, has been attacked by thinkers of wide influence within the Catholic family.

For the purposes of this book, these changes are important for their effect on unconventional religious tendencies within the Church. Have they been encouraged by the new climate, and have any groups come into being as expressions of them? Can they be looked on as essentially related to the impulses operative in the midst of very different traditions? These questions must inform our examination of new groups that have come into being both before and after the Second Vatican Council. Where has the unconventional believer stood in the past in the Roman Catholic tradition, and where does he stand now?

UNCONVENTIONAL BELIEF IN CATHOLIC TRADITION

The answer necessarily takes us beyond the workings of councils to the levels at which the authoritative decisions taken by the hierarchy either are put into effect or are evaded—that is, in the piety of ordinary believers, in their relations with their clergy, and in the quality of experience at the level of parish and diocese. Obviously, in an organization as wide-ranging as the Catholic Church, there is wide variation in piety and practice, but it must be said that in contrast to the image created by authoritarian pronouncements delivered in various historical circumstances, the Church has again and again made a place for unconventional believers and even for quasi-sectarian groups organized around particular religious visions. Examples include the religious orders founded from time to time, from the monastic Order of Saint Benedict, founded early in the sixth century, to the Dominican order of preachers and the Franciscans of the early thirteenth century, the Jesuits of the sixteenth century, and many less-well-known groups founded in more recent times. St. Francis of Assisi is a conspicuous case of a distinctly unconventional believer who came to be accepted and honored, and his point of view has been institutionalized among his followers within the overall structure of the Church.

It was, of course, more or less conscious policy of the Church to provide opportunities for individuals to pursue different versions of the truth so long as they remembered their obligations to the universal Church. We say only *more or less* conscious because until the Reformation the leaders of the Church had little reason to anticipate the formation of sectarian groups. Only the Waldensians of Italy, cast out of the Church late in the twelfth century, maintained an independence of any significance in the centuries before Martin Luther. Others paid the price of their lives for acting in such a way as to tear the seamless garment of the faith. Even after the Reformation, however, the Jesuits came into being as a militant order of priests, and other groups were founded for such good works as missions and teaching. In this period there was particular stress on recognizing a central authority in Rome.[3]

The major point, of course, is that in such groups people who in our terms should be considered unconventional believers submitted themselves to strenuous religious discipline under the supervision of Rome, and that they either isolated themselves from the everyday world or returned to it clearly identified by dress and behavior with a religious vocation. They may or may not have based their choice on a powerful religious experience; if such a gift were

3. For non-Catholic readers, a convenient introduction is Jaroslav Pelikan, *The Riddle of Roman Catholicism* (New York: Abingdon Press, 1959).

not granted them, they measured their own shortcomings and perhaps redoubled their religious efforts, for it was taken for granted
that the Church was the place within which the experience was to
be met. To take one example, Martin Luther as a young student is
said to have been frightened by a lightning bolt striking near him
as he crossed a field. His reaction was decisive: "St. Anne, I will become a monk." [4] In later days, such a response would not be auto-
matic. Nowadays many a sophisticated soul, feeling frightened by
such an event, would make an appointment to see a psychiatrist, and
the monk's vocation is discovered more indirectly.

Once again, we should not misinterpret even these aspects of the
history of the Catholic Church by concluding that the piety of ordinary people was not encouraged or was despised. It is true that the
most characteristic act of worship, the Mass, can be celebrated by a
priest with no congregation present, but as a congregational act it is
in some ways more conducive to personal religious experience than
much Protestant worship is. In the Mass there is not the Protestant
stress on paying attention, on hearing what is being said. Rather,
the believer is considered privileged to be present at the repetition
of an eternal mystery, and he may legitimately employ the occasion
for meditation, for such private prayer as the beads of the rosary
direct, and the like.

On the other hand, the very weight of tradition and the presence
of a hierarchical structure of authority put personal religious experience in a traditional context. Where so much stress is placed on
what might be called religious heroism, on the exemplary lives of
popes, saints, monks, priests, and nuns, the Catholic believer tends
naturally to interpret an intensification of his religious experience
as the impulse to a vocation within the Church. Short of that, one
trusts the institution for the fact that it embodies truth, and one
bends his conscience to it. One tends to refer the interpretation of
religious experience to professionals, who have been trained out of
the wealth of the tradition to hear a confession and to prescribe for
the pain caused by a moral dilemma. In this context the idea of
the religious sovereignty of the individual makes very little sense.

At least this is a substantially accurate sketch of the normal reactions of Catholics in the traditional Catholic milieu. We now may
look at several contemporary examples of unconventional religion
in a Catholic setting to see what has changed in the aftermath of the

4. This incident opens Roland H. Bainton's biography of Luther, *Here I
Stand* (New York: Mentor Books, 1955).

Second Vatican Council, which met in four extended sessions during the years 1962–65 and promulgated 16 documents dealing with every major aspect of the affairs of the Church.[5] It is fair to say that ideas associated with the words "renewal" and "relevance" were the common bases of recommendations in almost all areas except those where the Council fathers, in consultation with Vatican officials, were attempting to maintain a hierarchical authority. The liturgy was changed to encourage participation by all the people, and as was mentioned previously, several efforts were made to improve relations with non-Catholic Christians and even with followers of non-Christian religions.

With regard to the "renewal of religious communities," which in the Catholic vocabulary means cloisters, monasteries, and similar "set-apart" religious institutions, movement in the direction of modernization was encouraged. Archaic ways of dressing were replaced by those "suited to the circumstances of time and place." Most significantly, perhaps, there is in the document on the religious life a much more positive approach to the contemporary than earlier church documents would lead one to expect. "Lest the adaptations of religious life to the needs of our time be merely superficial," it reads, "religious should be properly instructed . . . in the prevailing manners of contemporary social life, and in its characteristic ways of feeling and thinking." [6] No doubt the intention behind these words was that the religious life would maintain the clarity of its appeal. The religious life would remain obviously superior to the layman's. Those who chose it would find themselves better equipped for what the Church calls their "apostolate" to the world, if they knew more about the contemporary through direct experience.

If in other respects, however, the Church were to give the impression of being much less sure of its truth, and if it were simultaneously to place a higher value than before on the religious possibilities of a layman's vocation, as in fact the council did do, might not the effect be a serious reduction in the attractiveness of the specialized religious vocations? The point is that the "characteristic ways of feeling and thinking" of the contemporary world include some firmly established ideas about religion, and they are rather widely at variance with Roman Catholic traditions, so that it is doubtful whether the Church could go much further toward an accommoda-

5. Walter M. Abbott, S.J., has published a convenient edition of *The Documents of Vatican II* (1966) under the imprint of The Guild Press, The America Press, and Association Press.

6. *Ibid.,* p. 479.

tion with modernity without losing the whole structure. Certainly radical Catholic thinking has not been satisfied by the changes in the Church; there has been a serious decline in the number of young people entering religious vocations; and it is possible to regard the work of Pope John as the opening of a Pandora's box, rather than a solution of the Roman Catholic confrontation with modernity.

CONTEMPORARY GROUPS

In such a climate as that created by Vatican II, religious innovations flourish. We may examine a few of them as possible indications of the place that unconventional believers may come to occupy in the Roman Catholic milieu in years to come. The spirit of renewal created in the Church, as may be imagined, a positive climate for a rich variety of experiments, particularly in activities that would draw lay participation. There were precedents in groups that had been permitted or encouraged in previous years. Early in the century, for example, under the general heading of Catholic Action, groups of European peasants and workers were organized to represent the interests of these groups and to increase the influence of the Church's position on social questions. In general these groups were under the leadership of clergymen and assumed the traditional presence of the Church as an important factor in the social life of the countries concerned.[7] In the case of the worker-priests of France, however, the authorities were not so encouraging, because these priests proceeded from the realization that most French workers were estranged from the Church and could be approached only by men who worked alongside them and shared their experiences and in this manner minimized their role as priests.

Such groups did not consider the possibility that the conditions of modern life moved people generally in the direction of a much more inward and self-generated spiritual life, but there were those who saw the need to create organizations directed toward this end as well. The most significant groups of this kind originated in Spain, which in modern times has given rise to much of the most deeply felt Catholic piety. In 1928 a group known as Opus Dei ("God's Work") was founded in Madrid. Since its official approval in 1950, it has been established in many parts of the world, particularly where

7. For information on Catholic Action and related movements, see the revised edition of Williston Walker, *A History of the Christian Church* (New York: Charles Scribner's Sons, 1959), pp. 525ff.

Spanish culture is strong.[8] Its members are mostly laymen, although priests may join. The group strongly encourages a deeper spirituality and an apostolic approach to others in all walks of life. The organization has focused much attention on educated people; it works among students and has founded a number of educational institutions. From time to time critics intimate that Opus Dei functions as a semisecret religious brotherhood (or sisterhood, since there is also a women's branch), occasionally acting as a kind of pressure group in political as well as religious matters.

Such suggestions really pertain to situations in which the Catholic Church has a virtual monopoly of organized religious activity and considerable influence over people at the centers of power. Thus whether or not Opus Dei has a self-conscious political program in countries like Spain or in any of the Latin American countries in which the Church is a power to be reckoned with, such intentions could not possibly have the same meaning where relatively few Catholics occupy positions of importance in government. In America, therefore, the group does not provoke many such suspicions, and there is no evidence that it merits them. In America it is an organization involving only a small number of individuals dedicated to systematic service of the will of God.

What is distinctive about Opus Dei, according to one of its best informed representatives in this country, is that the organization encourages people to make hard work an end in itself. It encourages a kind of layman's version of the ascetic discipline that the Church traditionally reserved for people leading the strictly religious life. The organization runs a secondary school of its own and such other enterprises as a residence house for students near Columbia University in New York City, a place where young people who need not be members of the group may experience a well-ordered environment in which self-discipline is encouraged. The students live in single rooms but eat together and attend worship in an attractive chapel in the house.

The founder and first President General of Opus Dei, Monsignor Escrivá de Balaguer, instituted the procedure by which new members indicated their commitment to the group by means of a personal letter to him in Rome. American members, who want to interpret the meaning of the group in the light of the religious differences that divide not only Catholics from other Christians but liberal from

8. Opus Dei has been reported on in a fragmentary way in the press. In 1968 Scepter Books of Dublin published a set of interviews entitled *Conversations with Monsignor Escrivá de Balaguer*. See articles in Catholic periodicals such as *Catholic Mind* in 1970 and 1971.

conservative Catholics, are apt to stress the practical emphasis of a commitment to Opus Dei. For them the stress on disciplined work and a well-ordered life is a solvent to the barriers of doctrinal difference, and a corrective to what many have seen as overemphasis on otherworldliness in the Catholicism of the days before Vatican II.

As a religiously oriented social organization, Opus Dei has predecessors in the Protestant milieu. After all, the motto for the ecumenical efforts that gave rise to the World Council of Churches was "Doctrine divides, but service unites"; this slogan owes much to the lesson of American experience, which was based on the need of our various religious groups to put aside differences of belief when faced with a common task. But the unhappy truth is that the importance of ideas cannot be so easily disregarded for the sake of harmony. If it is, you soon come to have an organization that has lost its reason for being. It turns out that service unites only when it is uncontroversial, or when it is expressed in one of the forms of traditional charity. Protestant groups that have defined service as the quest for social justice, for example, have often stirred up hornets' nests of opposition. But there is no evidence that Opus Dei intends to stir up controversy by its activity in America. Thus though what it provides may seem a rather new possibility for many Catholics, the organization remains an unconventional option for them within the framework of the Church rather than the divisive separate group it might become among Protestants.

What is distinctive about Opus Dei, of course, is the fraternal spirit fostered by the personal relation to the President General and the structure of authority that this implies. The closest parallel among Protestant groups might be Moral Re-Armament, which probably will not be able to recapture the influence it wielded during the lifetime of its founder, Frank Buchman, an American clergyman of Lutheran background who died in 1960.[9] The official name of his organization was the Oxford Group Movement, because it did very effective work among university students in England before World War II. It offers an instructive comparison with Opus Dei in terms of the ways in which unconventional religious activity has been organized in the past under Protestant and Catholic auspices. Both groups have concentrated much of their effort on people who are likely to be influential, by virtue of educational attainment or class position. Both provide a social group devoted to basically re-

9. See chapter on the Oxford Group Movement in Charles Braden, *Those Also Believe* (New York: Charles Scribner's Sons, 1949).

ligious ends but not closely linked to a local church organization. Their practical and "this-worldly" emphasis helps give support and a sense of solidarity to people troubled by the moral aspects of their involvement in business and professional careers. The support of such people in turn answers the question of how the group will be financed.

But a conspicuous difference of emphasis may be noted in the operations of the two groups. The basic technique of Moral Re-Armament in its early days was to organize house parties at which people discussed religious questions and made commitments to the group in an atmosphere of informality. As was the case in many similar Protestant efforts, denominational differences were minimized, and participation was supplementary in most cases to the more obviously religious pursuits of church membership. You joined MRA because you wanted a more direct and practical application of your faith than you received in church, and you met in the organization people from a variety of religious backgrounds who thought the same way you did. But you did not found a new church or denomination with them, and the personal bond between you and Frank Buchman was based on a model of fraternity and friendship. Though Moral Re-Armament continues, among other activities, sponsoring the touring musical presentation called "Up With People," it is probably accurate to say that the kind of interest it mobilized a generation ago has, for the most part, gone elsewhere. In particular, it has been replaced by efforts with a more social concern; an example is the Ecumenical Institute, which we shall examine below.

We may predict that Opus Dei will not become a significant movement in America. True, its fraternal bonds are more clearly religious than those of Moral Re-Armament, and in the present situation that is an advantage to the extent that people are looking for genuinely religious alternatives. But its appeal is too limited. It is intentionally an elite group, and though participation may have a profound effect on a relatively small number of individuals, their collective influence is not likely to be great. It has a disadvantage in holding up for admiration a type of character that is not as widely admired as used to be the case in the dominant Protestant culture, and a particular disadvantage in its taking for granted a very traditional idea of Catholic authority at a time when that idea has come very much into question. Since so much of its attention is given to the rational ordering of the behavior of a spiritual elite in traditional obedience to direction from Rome, it is not the milieu for

expression of the intensely religious strivings of many other contemporary American Catholics. New needs require a newer form.

NEW FORMS FOR NEW NEEDS

Another movement derived from a Spanish precedent may provide
us with a better case. It is the movement that organizes *cursillos de
cristianidad* ("little courses in Christianity") for people of many
different backgrounds, both priests and laymen. The Cursillo Movement began at about the end of World War II under the auspices
of the recently appointed bishop of Majorca, Juan Hervas y Benet.[10]
The *cursillo* centers around a weekend retreat during which the participants learn to take seriously both each other and the deeper
dimensions of their faith. Often the experience makes a deep impression on the participants and creates lasting friendships and commitments to Christian service.

The intention runs deeper than this, however. Literature of the
movement, which in the years since Vatican II has spread widely in
the United States and in other countries and has acquired a publishing center and a national secretariat, suggests the gradual emergence of a particular self-consciousness among those closely connected with the cursillo idea. Interestingly enough, the early movement was an adjunct of Catholic Action and helped strengthen it on
Majorca and in parts of Spain where cursillos were successful. Later
on it was decided to separate them again. Leaders of the Cursillo
Movement stress the importance of what is called the *ultreya,* group
meetings that follow up the cursillo and sometimes bring members
of the original cursillo groups together for reunions. By this process
the new religious motivation is to be utilized for the service of the
Church, and the movement is understood as a strategy for "changing
the world." But in contrast to Catholic Action, the cursillo point of
view came to focus on discovering and teaching by experience "what
is fundamental to being a Christian and structuring Christian life."
Its method directs itself to changing individuals and trusts them to
make a difference socially as they live out their lives.

It is apparent that the Cursillo Movement makes it possible for
the Catholic unconventional believer to give expression to his zeal.
Indeed it makes central the cultivation of an authentically religious

10. Starting in 1967 the Cursillo Movement published its own literature,
including a journal, *The Cursillo Movement,* using Box 304, Reno, Nevada
89504 as a mailing address.

inwardness among people who have not known such experience. Moreover, the suggestion is more than once made that Catholics not attuned to the need for deeper experience are simply those whose religious mentality was formed prior to Vatican II; the cursillo may thus be presented as a primary instrument of renewal of the Church in the new times. On the other hand, many echoes of traditional Catholic concerns are sounded in official literature of the national secretariat. It stresses that the effective cursillo is part of an overall parish plan, that its effectiveness derives from long practice in the methods employed in conducting the cursillo, that it is not to be judged by feelings of momentary exaltation but by the order that sustains the experience and transforms its original insights into a long-term Christian commitment. Priests are reminded of their key role at critical moments during the cursillo weekend and later as they exercise their role as spiritual directors of those whose faith has been quickened by the experience. In contrast to the many other means of "formation" or training that are commonplace in the Church, the cursillo concentrates on fundamental motivation—on head, heart, and will—but it is clear that the ordinary expectation is that priests will initiate the movement, select candidates, and evaluate the results. Church authority blesses the movement and utilizes it as a vehicle for its new intentions.

Does this mean that the Church can weather the storm of change, and that the intrinsically divisive tendencies in unconventional belief do not come to the fore in the Catholic milieu? It would be foolish to suggest this, when on all sides we read reports of far more radical initiatives on the part of both clergy and laity—the informal Masses of the so-called "underground church," the civil disobedience of priests and nuns in opposition to war and racial injustice, and repeated warnings that expectations aroused by Vatican II have run far beyond what the Church has thus far been willing to grant. Under the circumstances the question can just as well be reversed to ask whether the Cursillo Movement will persist and continue to prosper or become a way station to something else.

A final answer to this question depends on too many factors to be predictable, and doubtless it will not be the same for the different countries in which the Church and the movement have been important. The renewal impulse continues strong, and the legitimacy of the authority of the Church to prevent radical innovation is so widely questioned that much is permitted and occasionally even encouraged by the hierarchy that not many years ago would have caused scandal and been condemned. Many American Catholics, however, for the sake of a vivid experience of renewal, join groups whose members realize that they are violating Church regulations by ignoring parish boundaries, by making unauthorized changes in the liturgy of the Mass, and by doing so under the leadership of a priest who risks being disciplined but is willing to undergo the risk because of his commitment to renewal. Who can say how important is the excitement of doing what one does in such efforts *because* it is against the rules? In any case, the justification is the individual's religious autonomy, the sense of liberation derived from sharing doubts with others who were afraid to express them before.

Such a person, it is said, "wants freedom to search for what is relevant in the ancient truths and freedom to jettison what is obsolete." [11] The priest who wrote these words also expressed the fear that the religious alienation that produced the so-called "underground church" would not long be satisfied by guitar masses, folk-singing informality, and the exchange of religious uncertainties. He argued that the faithful who had committed themselves to such groups wanted to come into the open as good Catholics accepted by the Church hierarchy, but that if this did not happen soon, "the very best and most committed people" would simply be lost to the Church. Whether he is right or wrong, what is interesting about his description, for our purposes, is that it embodies many of the assumptions that give rise to sectarian development. In the eyes of those who belong to the underground Church, the best and most committed people are selected out of the Church for this movement, much as the Puritan "saints" were during the English Reformation. They take the faith seriously and are impatient at associating any longer with those who seem less ardent than they are. What cements their bonds is a shared religious experience that is rooted in but later threatens to break out of the conventions of the traditional liturgy. Their new loyalties lead them to make impossible demands of the traditional institution, which has obligations not only to them but also to Catholics who perceive the truth differently. What official of the Church, after all, could possibly give people freedom to decide for themselves what is obsolete and to jettison it, especially where fashions change as rapidly as they do in America? These demands are understandable, but so is the response, and so it is a real possibility that some members of the Catholic "underground" will leave the Church and become a sectarian group.

If the potentiality expressed in the underground church were to be realized, it could produce a number of results—a completely

---

11. Malcolm Boyd, ed., *The Underground Church* (Baltimore: Penguin Books, 1969), p. 135.

transformed Catholic Church, which is unlikely; a movement of people out of the Church and into existing Protestant churches or into no church at all; perhaps the founding of a new sectarian group that will retain the Mass but change almost everything else. Until we see the actual outcome, we are reduced to projecting current trends such as decline in church attendance and religious vocations, the closing of parochial schools because of rising costs and lack of religious professionals to staff them, defections from the ranks of priests and nuns, and the like. This procedure has little to recommend it, for such trends do not continue indefinitely and probably respond in large measure to events that cannot be foreseen.

CHARISMATIC RENEWAL

What we may learn more from, therefore, is a Catholic group linked to a recognizable organization but less traditionally so than the Cursillo Movement—a group whose members are concerned particularly with religious experience and personal assurance in faith. Such a group is the charismatic renewal movement, whose members are otherwise known as Catholic Pentecostals.[12] This movement is not an imported renewal strategy, but a rather spontaneous response of some American Catholics to the realization that their religious experience has lacked depth of feeling. In its growth the movement has found it profitable to be open to insights from the non-Catholic tradition of Pentecostalism, and it is marked by a high degree of lay initiative and leadership.

The distinctive flavor of charismatic renewal may best be explained here by description of its style of worship, which is here contrasted with the more conventional Catholic ritual for the benefit of non-Catholic readers. The regular Catholic Mass is a highly traditional ceremony enacted under an explicit set of ritual prescriptions symbolically linking every word and gesture to Catholic tradition and theology. In essence the Mass is a symbolic reenactment of the death of Christ, interpreted as a sacrificial offering to God on behalf of sinners. In stepping to the altar of the sacrifice, the priest becomes identified with Christ in his role as symbolic High Priest on man's behalf. Since Christ is God become man, Christ takes the initiative that man has no right to assume on his own behalf; by a central

12. For information on Catholic Pentecostalism, see Edward D. O'Connor, C.S.C., *The Pentecostal Movement* (Notre Dame, Ind.: Ave Maria Press, 1971). A more personal account is *Catholic Pentecostals*, by Kevin and Dorothy Ranaghan (Paramus, N.J.: Paulist Press, 1969).

paradox of the faith Christ also presents himself as a sacrificial victim, the "lamb of God," doing so again because man has nothing to offer in his own right and on his own behalf. Because of the merit won by Christ through this action, worshipers may hope to be saved through him. As a holy mystery, the ceremony may quite appropriately be embellished with rich vestments, music, and expensive utensils and altar furnishings; and it need not be wholly understood to be deeply impressive.

The believer may relate to this ceremony in several ways, all of which he understands as making him part of the Christian community. He may be inspired and instructed by the recital of prayers, the reading of the Scriptures, and the transformation of the elements of bread and wine into the body and blood of Christ. He may observe the liturgical drama as having no very immediate reference to his spiritual state but as a religious obligation and as a source of solace when the time comes that he needs it. He may fulfill the higher obligation at least once a year to receive communion and to prepare himself for so doing by confessing his sins to the priest and receiving absolution along with accepting spiritual discipline. But the basic strength of the traditional understanding of the Mass is that the events and their meaning are factual and true, historically and eternally, as an objective order of reality for the Catholic consciousness and a perennial resource.

In practice, as well as by way of many implications of the traditional theory, the involvement of laymen in the ceremony of the Mass was and still is often perfunctory, much more passive than active. Usually churches are large and crowded, so that the rite may seem only a spectacle. In addition, because of the requirement of confession before reception of the communion elements, on most occasions the believer is not able to regard himself as a full participant in the proceedings, because he has not been absolved of his sins. Confession itself seems generally to be declining, perhaps because its secrecy seems impersonal or because the working definitions of sin do not correspond to the contemporary situation. This is a source of difficulty particularly for the clergy, who are not content to be simply correct performers of the traditional rite. They see their identity validated to the extent that they can get people involved at a deeper level of spirituality.

Many of these concerns were expressed in the work of Vatican II. One of the major difficulties it tried to meet was what was felt to be widespread ignorance of what was really taking place in the ceremony; to men steeped in the Catholic educational tradition, to understand was to respond. Accordingly, the Second Vatican Council gave much attention to liturgical changes that would increase the understanding of laymen and decrease the symbolic distance between them and the clergy. One result is that the altar was detached from the wall, and now the priest stands behind it facing the congregation. Particular importance was attached to translating many parts of the service into the people's own language for the sake of intelligibility. Discretion was given to bishops to allow their priests to give people the wine in communion as well as the bread. Since the Middle Ages only priests had drunk the wine. Probably this was on account of fear that the wine would be spilled, therefore that the blood of Christ would be profaned. The bread was regarded as standing for both elements of communion, but in democratic times such discrimination is resented. In addition, transubstantiation, the doctrine explaining how the bread and wine become the body and blood of Christ, is probably understood less magically by most believers than it used to be. The intention is that by receiving both elements they become more deeply involved in the ceremony.

These changes were widely applauded and quickly put into effect by most bishops on instruction from the appropriate office in Rome, but it is difficult to imagine that the changes would make any important difference except to those who already knew and responded deeply to the traditional form. Consider therefore the implications of an alternative form of Catholic worship, a pentecostal prayer group. A number of people, most of whom are known to each other, gather in a room of suitable size at an appointed hour but with no clear agreement on when the service will end or just what will happen during it. There is the expectation, however, of deep feeling and perhaps also of the manifestation of what are known as "spiritual gifts," which have a scriptural basis in the epistles of St. Paul and include healing, preaching, prophesying, and "speaking in tongues." The last item, whose technical name is the Greek word "glossolalia," is the more or less unintentional utterance of sounds meaningless to the speaker and usually to hearers as well.[13] It is a much more central feature in the old Protestant tradition of Pentecostalism than it is in these meetings, but it still is a highly desired experience.

The service may be begun by a leader giving instruction or encouragement, especially if newcomers are present. Typically the leader is not a priest. Perhaps there is a feeling that the leader should not be a priest, given the way in which most Catholics look to the religious for leadership—whereas they should do more for

13. See William J. Samarin, "Glossolalia," *Psychology Today*, VI,3 (August 1972), 48ff.

themselves, to this way of thinking. Thus in charismatic renewal services there may be a team of leaders, women as well as men, and the service may start with folk songs or hymns that people can be expected to know and join in singing. There is no prescribed order of worship except that provided by a particular leader. By pre-arrangement, but also by spontaneous individual decision, various individuals lead in prayer, speak exhortations or give witness to the power of their own religious experience, read portions of the Scriptures that strike them as relevant to the occasion, or encourage the group to sing together. Leadership and planning are not lacking, but they are exercised by attunement to what the moment calls for, by a tone of sincerity and conviction and a spirit of warm acceptance. There is much unstructured prayer, silent as well as spoken. The silence is alive with the shared hope for the spiritual gifts, and the effect of such powerful expectations can be very much more deep and personal than what happens in attendance at the Mass. Another factor is what we have spoken of previously as human scale. The charismatic renewal meetings may reach a hundred or more on a regular weekly basis. Indeed, annual national conventions have brought together a thousand or more of the many thousands of people who have had intensive contact with the movement. But the local groups, which are the heart of the movement, consist of people who make an effort, or who perhaps find it easy, to know one another and to welcome newcomers. The sense of a genuinely caring community is central to the experience.

No doubt there are many who find such worship congenial for reasons of personality and without serious regard for its implications for religious tradition. Indeed, there is a kind of social network of people who seek out this kind of worship no matter what the denominational auspices under which it is conducted. The interest in charismatic renewal brings together many people across denominational boundaries and thus poses the possibility that this mode of worship may be the basis for a new religious group. On the other hand, where a group is Catholic, there is concern for the problem of Catholic renewal and, as always in Catholic circles, for a theological justification that will keep the movement in touch with the Catholic tradition.

Since the Catholic Pentecostal movement began at a university, Duquesne, and continues to be important at Notre Dame and particularly at Ann Arbor, Mich., among members of the state university community, it cannot be said to be a purely emotional or anti-intellectual movement. Some of the leaders of the Ann Arbor group in the late sixties and early seventies were formerly identified

with the Cursillo Movement, and some priests have received episcopal approval to initiate charismatic groups within the regular
diocesan structure. Does all this mean that they will be accommodated to the conventional Church and provide a place for unconventional Catholic believers without serious disruption?

The answer may well lie in the implications of the central imagery
of the movement, the symbols that link theology and experience and
that participants use in their thinking and in their communication
with each other in order to interpret religiously what they are doing.
Thus the movement is charismatic because, as the original Greek
word implies, it has to do with freely given gifts. In New Testament
terms the agent of these gifts is the Holy Spirit, who, "between the
times," as the theological language goes—that is, between the historical career of Christ and his second coming and therefore during
our lifetimes—remains as the bearer of God's grace. It is undoubtedly the promise of these spiritual gifts, and the conviction that
they have been manifested, that pentecostals of all persuasions take
to be the foundations of their faith and practice.

Who receives the gifts, though, and just how does one know that
they have been received? The Catholic implications of these questions pose many problems for the Church of the tradition. The crux
of the difficulty lies in the fact that spiritual gifts are received in an
experience called the "baptism of the Holy Spirit." The word "experience" is used advisedly, because spirit-baptism is validated inter-
nally, not by the external test of speaking with tongues. It can be
dissembled, certainly, and one may be self-deceived that he has the
gift out of zeal to receive it, but to have it is to *know*. It comes with
power, and one may then sing, or speak with tongues, or prophesy,
but the spirit-baptism, to those who testify that they have had it, is
the *sine qua non* of true religious experience. Significantly, in the
Ann Arbor group there has been a distinction between people on
the basis of the baptism, one meeting being held for those who have
been so baptized and, on a different evening, a meeting open also to
interested members of the public.

In a formal sense this distinction is very similar to the division
of the service of the Mass into the part intended for catechumens,
those not yet confirmed in full membership, and the so-called
"mass of the faithful," which is the communion service proper. And
that is just the point, for the Catholic Church is founded on the
conviction that it has the power itself to give gifts of the spirit, and
to empower its clergy to do so through a valid ceremony of ordination, following New Testament references to which it attributes critical importance. Charisma according to this point of view is what

the German sociologist Max Weber called "charisma of office." [14] It has a certain historical and even a psychological validity, for accepting it as part of an objective order of things, like the truth of the Mass, has sustained the work of many a priest who was unsure of himself as a person.

But to the spirit-filled layman, and to the really anxious priest, perhaps, the true charisma is more like what the word has come to mean in popular usage—a personal force of character or manner that gives evidence of a vital internal power of direction. A priest may have it, but to become a priest gives no guarantee that one has or ever will have it. This being the case, for Catholic Pentecostals whether to maintain a close tie to the Church must remain an open question, but there is little reason to predict that a sectarian development is inevitable among them. Many find that traditional liturgy has been transformed for them into a rich and vital experience, even when the service has not been modernized in accord with the rubrics of the period after the Second Vatican Council. What continues to move them is a clearly religious experience with an honored tradition in the Church. So long as the Church provides a milieu for such experience and allows it to be defined as Catholic, it will provide a real answer to a contemporary need.

RADICAL SOCIAL ACTION

By contrast, let us look finally at the kind of contemporary answer that has received a lot more attention in the media. There are many members of the Catholic Church (just as there are many from the several Protestant denominations) for whom radical social action and the quest for social justice have become the true modern hallmarks of a vital faith, and for whom traditional Catholicism with its conservative leadership has become well-nigh intolerable. Much of this feeling surfaced in the sixties during the civil rights movement. As an example, one priest, Father Joseph Groppi, became famous (some would say notorious) for leading marches in Milwaukee in support of equal rights for blacks in housing. Efforts that received less publicity were made on behalf of blacks in Louisiana, and individual priests and nuns made their witness at Selma, Alabama, and elsewhere by taking part in civil rights demonstrations.

As the civil rights movement blended with the movement to op-

14. The original discussion of charismatic authority is in Max Weber, *The Theory of Social and Economic Organization*, ed. by Talcott Parsons (New York: The Free Press, 1964).

pose the war in Southeast Asia, some who ardently objected to the way things were going in America expressed their feeling by what one author called "divine disobedience." [15] The best-known members of this group of Catholics were Daniel Berrigan, a Jesuit priest, and his brother Philip, a member of another order of priests. Associated with their efforts were both laypeople and "religious," both men and women, both Protestants and Catholics. Dramatizing their opposition to the war, small groups of those associated with this position broke into local draft boards and defaced draft records on several occasions. The Berrigans decided not to follow one tradition of civil disobedience and take the resulting punishment passively, but to elude capture in order to make a symbolic statement denying all legitimacy to the authorities putting them on trial. After a time they were found, tried, convicted, and committed to prison. They were subsequently harassed further for smuggling written materials out to their followers and for discussing a rather far-fetched plan to explode bombs in federal buildings and kidnap a high official of the Nixon administration.

It is difficult to know how serious such plotting was on the basis of newspaper articles. There is better material for understanding these efforts in works published by the participants themselves. Daniel Berrigan, for example, dramatized his case by writing a play about his trial, a play that was successfully produced in New York City and was subsequently made into a film starring no less a celebrity than Gregory Peck. It is conceivable that by such means the Berrigans and their point of view became better known to the general public than to most members of their own church, in which their position has not yet predominated. Will their viewpoint become dominant in the Church?

To find an answer, one may have to look to the wider field of public opinion in which the Berrigans have sought to exert influence on the post-Vatican II generation of Catholics and non-Catholics. Daniel Berrigan's play, "The Trial of the Catonsville Nine," [16] came at a time when religious concerns were once more in vogue. Rock music frankly confessed its debt to the Negro spiritual and to old-line Protestant gospel singing, and so the way was prepared for spectacular productions like "Jesus Christ Superstar." In the field of popular entertainment it did not seem altogether incongruous that a celebrated musician from a secular Jewish background

15. The phrase is the title of a book by Francine D. Gray (New York: Vintage Books, 1971).

16. See Daniel Berrigan, *The Trial of the Catonsville Nine* (Boston: Beacon Press, 1970).

should compose a Mass for the dedication of a national Arts Center to the memory of the first Roman Catholic president of the country. The loosening of the hold of tradition in all aspects of Catholic culture in America had another expression in the colorful art of Corita Kent, one of many nuns who left the Church, and in the grateful response of the many Catholics and non-Catholics who found her work appealing.

These are several examples of the fact that in contemporary culture what is noticed and reported on becomes, for that reason alone, something which figures in the decisions of countless people who want both to be part of the world they live in, the contemporary world, and at the same time true to their faith. Since in the days following Vatican II the Church had set itself in the direction of renewal, anything that presented itself as innovative commanded attention if it had any good qualities at all, and perhaps in some cases even it had none at all. On the other hand, in order to be consequential for the Church, any such event must generate a group with some staying power if it is to be a reliable milieu for the unconventional believer. That is, renewal and novelty are not the same. What is only novel does not last. And since American popular culture puts a premium on novelty, any attempt to communicate religious truth through popular art forms is unlikely to have lasting importance for religious institutions.

Is this to be, in retrospect, the verdict on the work of the Berrigans and what they represent in general, even apart from the dramatization of their trial? It is certainly true that the quest for social justice is no fad in the Christian (or, for that matter, in the Jewish) tradition; this quest has had an honored place since the time of the teachings of the prophets of the Old Testament, and it is presented as a more valid alternative to much of what passes for faith in the institutions of conventional religion. A much quoted passage from the prophet Amos, for example, attributes to God the following words:

> I hate, I despise your feasts,
>   and I take no delight in your solemn assemblies . . .

> Take away from me the noise of your songs;
>   to the melody of your harps I will not listen.
> But let justice roll down like waters,
>   and righteousness like an ever-flowing stream.
>
> (*Amos* 5:21, 23–24 RSV)

This prophetic stance has long been an attractive model for liberally trained clergymen of the mainline Protestant denominations. It was not so often a model for priests until the aftermath of Vatican II, but in the new atmosphere of renewal it has become much more appropriate, even if not yet commonplace.

On the other hand, the passion for social justice can lead to bitter disillusionment with the traditional ways of the Church—so much so that for many reform-minded Protestants at least the power and resources for change possessed by secular social agencies have come to seem much more attractive options than what is available through the various churches. In other words, the prophet often finds it so difficult to discover a sympathetic audience in the Church that he either changes his views or ends up going elsewhere to work for change. There is some evidence that zeal for social justice often arises as a substitute for a lost or declining religious faith.[17] For such people, no possible reforms serve the cause of justice clearly enough to redeem the traditional churches, and to become part of the "underground church" previously mentioned becomes a station on the way out.

There is a curious similarity on this score between Daniel Berrigan's play and Leonard Bernstein's Mass. In a dramatic moment Bernstein shows the vessels that contain the elements of the communion borne ever higher to escape the clamor of the crowd crying for peace, only at last to be dashed to fragments when it appears that no such escape is possible. In Berrigan's case two episodes of destruction of draft records are compared. In the first, the files are covered with blood, which means that a Christian redemption is possible. In the second, they are burned with homemade napalm in a much more secular gesture, using a more contemporary but less Christian symbol. The second moves toward a point similar to Bernstein's, that the Church has little or nothing to offer to the crying needs of the present day. But it may also be that in the perspective of a few years' time neither image will have been of much consequence for the Church, even for its unconventional believers.

A TRADITIONAL CASE

This may be asserted with all the more confidence because effective work for social justice need not be wedded to criticism or rejection of the traditions of the faith. One good example is a long-established but still very vital association of unconventional be-

---

17. See Charles Y. Glock and Rodney Stark, *Religion and Society in Tension* (Chicago: Rand McNally & Company, 1965).

lievers existing under informal Catholic auspices, a movement called The Catholic Worker.[18] The movement is identified with a remarkable woman named Dorothy Day. Raised in a family of newspapermen, and converted from the Episcopal faith as a young woman, Dorothy Day associated herself with a man named Peter Maurin in the publication of an eloquent newspaper that carries the name of the movement and in 1973 began its thirty-ninth volume. Miss Day has sustained the effort since the death of Maurin by extraordinary personal dedication and the help of a devoted group of supporters, Catholic and non-Catholic. For 25 cents a year, the nominal price of a subscription to *The Catholic Worker,* you can get some insight into an effort that has many dimensions. The *Worker* makes an eloquent plea for socialism, maintains a house of refuge and rehabilitation near the Bowery in New York City for derelicts, serves as a center for lively inquiry into the connections between faith and the things of this world, and provides a link to several farms in country locations where the movement's members can get their bearings by working with their hands in contact with nature.

One of the most significant aspects of The Catholic Worker movement is that the Mass is profoundly relevant as an almost constant source of deep spiritual vitality for members. They can work for change from within their version of the Church because it stands as a symbol of values that essentially don't change but have to be aspired to. Attempts to change the celebration of the Mass are not welcomed by such unconventional believers. On the contrary, they are apt to feel betrayed by change because for them the tradition lives as a result of their commitment to it. Will changing and adapting the faith to contemporary styles stimulate commitment to it? Or is the reverse true? It is difficult to say for certain, but Dorothy Day's example suggests that for some the Church is most effective by firmly sustaining its best traditions.

All these examples show some of the ways in which contemporary Catholics have expressed themselves as unconventional believers. There is no indication that the leaders of the Church will force any of its members into a sectarian existence, as might have been the case before the start of this century. But as even these brief descriptions should have made plain, each group bears its own implications for the future of the Church. Although the outcome of all such efforts cannot be known in advance, it seems a fair prediction that

18. For an anthology of articles from *The Catholic Worker,* see Thomas C. Cornell, *A Penny a Copy* (New York: The Macmillan Company, 1968).

some of the more radical efforts will have less effect on changing the Church than they seem to have at present.

One fundamental fact is the continued importance of the tradition of Catholic worship, particularly the Mass as conducted by a clergy ordained to this and to other specifically religious functions. While this basic structure of the faith is preserved, the Catholic Church will still be recognizable.

But is there any guarantee that the Church will remain recognizable in this way? That is hard to say, but the chances are good that it will. Contemporary thinkers are much less hostile to the mysteries of faith than were earlier critics in times when science seemed the answer to everything. In addition, the need to make worship more comprehensible seems much less pressing in an age when many think that the depth of liturgical symbolism is a counterpart to the depth of our psychological penetration into the workings of the human mind and spirit. In this milieu the Mass does not have to be understood to be appreciated even by highly sophisticated people.

What we have tried to demonstrate here is that while some unconventional expressions of the Catholic faith tend toward new and very different forms of worship and group life, by no means do all unconventional expressions do so. It is entirely plausible, perhaps even probable, that in years to come the new form of the Church, however rich and varied it seems, may be not so very different from the old. More importantly, the chances are good that the Roman Catholic Church of future years will continue to provide spiritual elbow-room for many expressions of the vigor of the unconventional believer.

The New Jew and the Old

It certainly seems justified to say, as Will Herberg did in the middle fifties, that Judaism has become an accepted part of American culture. One mark of this acceptance is the frequency with which we come across references to "Judaeo-Christian civilization," a phrase obviously indicating that the religious traditions have so much in common that they can be amalgamated into a single term covering both civilizations. Jews have made an impact on many significant aspects of American culture—especially in business, the professions, education, and the arts. They have achieved importance out of proportion to their numbers, for they are only about three percent of the population. Although still heavily concentrated in the major cities of the East, they have moved into the suburbs in recent years and thus have come closer to fitting the image of the movies, popular stories, and television shows, where the family lives in its own house and drives in a car to the local shopping center or goes on a vacation to the mountains. In religious terms what confirms the image best is the appearance of the synagogue or temple on equal terms with the church or the parochial school, with far greater acceptance than many a sectarian Protestant group, such as a church of the Holiness persuasion or a Jehovah's Witnesses Kingdom Hall.

Judaism became Americanized in the days of the large immigrations, to the degree that anti-Semitism, which was a familiar and ugly reality in former days in America, seems to have become an echo of the past rather than a significant living voice. This does not mean that Christian Americans understand the religion of Jews—

for the majority of Christian Americans are profoundly ignorant of many aspects of their own religion, as many a survey has demonstrated—but it does mean that Jews are not nearly so often perceived as aliens, to be discriminated against if their lineage becomes known. Vatican II had something to say in this respect by purging from Catholic teaching and prayer the old references to Jews as "perifidious" murderers of Christ. It is hard to say how much effect such teachings ever had, and it is therefore also a problem to know how important these changes of Vatican II were, but it now appears that at least formally Jews and Christians are free to follow their respective faiths in harmony.

An alternative way to say the same thing, perhaps more accurately, would be to say that Jews, like other formerly isolated minorities who have since become full members of American society, may now be in a position to have their religious tradition subjected to the same strains and pressures for change that have profoundly affected all other religions in America. How fares it with Judaism in these terms? It turns out that we can discover differences between conventional and unconventional religion among Jews, many of the same ones we have already noticed among Christians. There are also important dissimilarities, which reflect the fact that the religious experience of Jews is not the same as that of Christians. We need to start our examination, therefore, with an idea of what is different about Judaism in the modern world in order to understand how to evaluate what is happening to it today.

The most fundamental point, for those who are not familiar with Judaism, is that by comparison with Christianity it is a faith defined rather more by custom and practice, by a sense of communal belonging and family solidarity, than it is by definition of belief and faithfulness to religious doctrine.[1] Jewishness has been based on a tie of blood rather than membership—the traditional definition of a Jew has been one born of a Jewish mother. Jews lived for centuries in Europe in enforced isolation from the Christian population, in some places even being forcibly converted to Christianity while trying surreptitiously to preserve their identity. Jews learned under these circumstances to care for one another, and the crown of achievement

1. Judaism is, of course, an enormous subject, and many works are available on aspects of it. For readers unfamiliar with the subject, a good place to begin is *Judaism, A Portrait,* by Leon Roth (New York: The Viking Press, Inc., 1961). Two good books entitled *American Judaism* are by Nathan Glazer (Chicago: University of Chicago Press, 1957), a historical treatment, and Jacob Neusner (Englewood Cliffs, N. J.: Prentice-Hall, Inc., 1972), a more thematic work.

in their community was to become a master of its sacred traditions—
the biblical texts but particularly also the rich deposits of rabbinical
commentaries, which showed ways of making the old scriptural laws
live for them and thus reinforced the solidarity of the group. In
many places these legal traditions governed Jewish communities, so
that learning was a practical discipline as well as an art. For most
Christians the faith is no longer a binding code of behavior in all
aspects of life. Jews cannot feel this way.

Thus emancipation of the Jews, which officially began during the
French Revolution but proceeded only fitfully in other places there-
after, confronted Jews with a religious dilemma. In many places it
remained a disadvantage to be a Jew, but there were no longer overt
pressures to forswear the faith and convert to Christianity. At the
same time religious zeal was generally declining, and it became
increasingly less necessary to be a believer of any kind. In America
one was not automatically a church member and was not under great
social pressure to be so, at least not in the cities, where most Jews
lived. Many Jews found their religious commitment declining, especially when they lived far from other Jews. Thus the unity enforced
in former times by persecution ironically enough began to be lost
not long after the Jews had become free to worship openly according
to their traditions. Some ceased to practice their faith and even
found it possible to join Christian groups, especially when only a
perfunctory acceptance of Christian principles was required.

As we have already indicated, by tradition the communal aspect
of Judaism required conformity to a highly detailed code of behavior. This prescribed minutely even for such matters as dress,
length of hair, and food. It was especially necessary to avoid any
semblance of doing work on the Sabbath, which lasts from sundown
on Friday to sundown on Saturday. Orthodox Jews still observe
these rules very seriously; many of the rules, of course, are not
only onerous but often costly. What is perhaps the worst aspect of
the more visible of the 613 *mitzvot,* or commandments, which need
to be obeyed, is that unlike theological ideas they cannot easily be
modernized or compromised in order to make the faith more compatible with modern requirements.

When this dilemma became intensified among Jews, a religious
problem was posed more acutely than for Christians. Since an
acute logic had long been attuned to demonstrating how minute
infractions of the rules might be enough to invalidate the whole
effort to observe them, there was little room for halfway measures.
Either you keep kosher or you don't, for if the commandments were
truly given by God for the guidance of His people, who has the

authority to choose between those that are to be relinquished and those to be retained? In other words, in comparison to the Christian the Jew, in affirming his membership in his religious community, binds himself to a code of behavior justified not so much in terms of moral value as by virtue of the fact that it was given by God and communicated by Moses and the ancient rabbis to future generations.

This is not to say that Judaism is not also a religion of belief and moral responsibility. On the contrary, one of the strengths of the faith is that it depends on the informed participation of its adult male membership to a degree far surpassing what is generally required of Christians. The father of a family presides over the home ceremonies during the Passover season, and each member of the family has a role to play as well. In traditional Judaism a congregation is dependent not on the presence of a priest, clergyman, or preacher, but on a *minyan* (or quorum) of ten men who share in the conduct of worship. The rabbi is important primarily as an expert in interpreting the legal tradition. This helps explain why Judaism has depended so heavily on stressing learning for all. On the other hand, the stress on specifically Jewish patterns of behavior and their cultivation in the family setting is an indication of the reasons why Jews are so concerned with Jews' intermarriage, as opposed to the question of religious membership. You do not become a Jew by joining a synagogue; you *are* a Jew, and if you value the faith, to have a child marry into a Christian family is considered the same as losing that child.

These remarks suggest some of the important ways in which Judaism has been especially vulnerable in modern times, as well as some of the directions taken by those who have tried to create a Judaism more in touch with what they consider the modern spirit. If a vital Judaism has depended on assuring the learning of Hebrew and the study of rabbinic wisdom, the lack of such learning has been a perennial danger, since it makes impossible an authentic service of worship. In this respect several generations of American Jews have been impoverished, for their communities were few and scattered, and the supply of properly trained rabbis was inadequate until the twentieth century. If you could not worship rightly, either you or your children were likely to be lost to Judaism as effectively as if you married outside the faith. If you could not worship rightly you would be strongly tempted also to give up the dietary and sabbath laws, and thus you would begin to feel in your heart that you were no longer a Jew. These motifs can be seen in accounts of life among long-established groups of Jews of German (Ashkenazic) and Spanish or Portuguese (Sephardic) descent in the middle of the nineteenth century, when business and professional opportunities were making success possible for Jews in the mainstream of American life.

RELIGIOUS ASSIMILATION

Many other currents tended to assimilate Jews into American life, after which they ceased to be Jews at all.[2] For one thing, from colonial times there had been a strong sentiment among Christians to think of America as the new and the genuine Israel. In our own time it is difficult to realize how deeply felt this conviction was, but many a Jew responded warmly to the image of America as a free, liberating land. Isaac Mayer Wise, for example, the leader of the movement of Reform Judaism, said a century ago that "Every child born on this soil is Americanized. Our country has a peculiar people to work out a new and peculiar destiny." [3] He did not mean that he thought Americans were odd or queer, but that the country, and each of its citizens, had an important role to play in working out the destiny set by God for the New World. To be a Jew had somehow to be compatible with being an American also.

This in turn suggests a second and in many ways a more critical factor, the issue of truth as defined by science and rationality. To be an American implied a commitment to the modern and the progressive, and a corresponding rejection of what was old and merely traditional. Christian doctrine proved capable of adaptation. At least many Christians were convinced of this capability, and since Christian practice follows doctrinal changes, especially in providing a wide range of denominations for the expression of different understandings of the faith, Protestantism prospered in the American setting. Such developments posed a direct challenge to Judaism, however, especially to its legalistic code of behavior, based on revelation and the communal tradition of a group that had often been forced to live in ghettos. A particular focus of these concerns was the perennial dream of the reestablishment of Israel as a nation, a hope that seemed exceedingly vain during the nineteenth century.

Thus for many Jews the issue was set in terms of choosing between assimilation into Christian America or holding to loyalties that seemed thoroughly out of touch with the times. Under these

2. Assimilation is a central point of discussion in contemporary Judaism. See, for example, Chapter 3 of Neusner, *ibid.*

3. Quoted in Conrad Cherry, *God's New Israel* (Englewood Cliffs, N. J.: Prentice-Hall, Inc., 1971), p. 227.

circumstances it is altogether understandable that alternatives would arise, but also that they would be subject to particular difficulties in terms of the Jewish tradition. The unconventional alternatives of a century or more ago are reflected in the more familiar divisions of Judaism today.

Certainly what was done by Rabbi Wise and by others like him offered Jews new religious possibilities.[4] The Reform movement started in German-speaking countries in reaction to what seemed the irrational restrictiveness of the Orthodox tradition. Heavy German immigration to America in the years between 1836 and 1880 made German Jews numerically dominant among the Jewish minority, and they were able to call from German-speaking regions of Europe rabbis who were better educated than the leaders of the older Sephardic Orthodox groups in America, and who in many cases knew about the critical study of the Bible that was proceeding in Christian circles and would have important effects on denominational rivalries in America in later years. Wise came from Bohemia, where he violated restrictions on the number of Jewish weddings that one rabbi could perform. He found the American situation very gratifying. He and others like him changed the traditional worship to allow the use of English, a sermon, organ music and the singing of hymns, choirs, and the like. Women did not have to be segregated but could sit with their husbands and sons. Traditional themes like prayers for the restoration of Israel were omitted from the liturgy books, which came to be used increasingly in Reform congregations. The Jewish people were to think of themselves not as exiled from their homeland because of sinfulness but as a people with a mission.

This mission, of course, was conceived by Reform Judaism in terms of those aspects of the tradition that seemed most in touch with the modern, especially with progressive America. Standards of rationality and the ethical vision of the prophets were the major themes stressed as the true heritage of Israel. As a new emphasis in Judaism, this point of view was exciting and provided the basis for unconventional believers among Jews of that day to feel themselves part of a dynamic religious movement. Reform temples of today do not always give this impression, and they certainly do not seem to give scope for unconventional believers to find a satisfying expression of their religious interests. Why is this the case? For one thing, the point of view expressed in Reform Judaism was very

4. For information on the life of Isaac Mayer Wise, see Israel Knox, *Rabbi in America, the Story of Isaac M. Wise* (Boston: Little, Brown and Company, 1957).

much bound to the times and lost luster as the twentieth century revealed the serious weaknesses of Enlightenment rationalism. Similarly, such views by their nature do not stimulate a strong emotional commitment. They are liberating to people who have grown up under authoritative and repressive control, but to the children of such people they may seem only bland. They had so much in common with similar views held in the Unitarian Church, for example, that they did not seem compatible with maintaining a Jewish identity. Thus some former Reform Jews organized the Ethical Culture Society in New York City in 1876,[5] while others joined the so-called "community churches," in company with former members of various Christian denominations.

CONSERVATIVE JUDAISM

For congregations that maintained their Reform associations, in more recent times the problem has been to try to understand what it means to be a Jew in the modern world. Many such Jews have moved toward the third major division of Judaism, the Conservative movement, which is in many ways a specifically American response to the question of the modern Jewish identity. What brought this movement into being was a combination of the discomfort felt by many pious Jews, particularly those of Sephardic background, at the radical transformations of the faith in German Reform circles, and the upheaval caused by the enormous growth of Jewish immigration to the United States in the 40-year period beginning in 1881. Russian persecution of the Jews sent half a million or more Jews to America in the final two decades of the century—twice as many as the total Jewish population in the United States at the start of the period. These Jews had lived very much to themselves and very intensely followed their faith in many cases. Those of them who abandoned it became political and social radicals rather than stopping at such halfway measures as Reform provided. Many of them were so poor as to threaten the position that had been won by the enterprising German Jews of former generations.

The response that generated the Conservative movement was centered around an educational institution, as one might expect.[6] The

5. The founder of the Ethical Culture Society was Felix Adler, son of a Reform rabbi. See David Muzzey, *Ethics as a Religion* (New York: Simon and Schuster, Inc., 1951).

6. For information on the history of Conservative Judaism, see Moshe Davis, *The Emergence of Conservative Judaism* (New York: Burning Bush Press, 1963).

Jewish Theological Seminary began offering classes in New York City in 1887, but it did not prosper until after the turn of the century, when large contributions, in many cases from well-to-do Reform Jews, created a suitable endowment and attracted first-rate scholars to the institution. In this effort was present the self-conscious intention to provide well-educated rabbis for the recent immigrants, rabbis who would bring a measure of decorum to the often noisy bustle of an Orthodox synagogue service and in the process help instruct the foreign-born in the alien ways of America. For some of the men who gave money out of self-interested motives, rather than religious ones, the idea seemed to be that an anti-Semitic reaction could be avoided if the East European immigrants were quickly Americanized.

But the growth of any minority to a certain number makes it possible for the members of that minority to form a genuine community. Thus the settlement of ultimately millions of Jews, particularly in New York City, created the possibility for a Jewish subculture to develop that might resist Americanization. This subculture had its own schools, its own food stores and restaurants, its own newspapers, even a special language, Yiddish, a variant of German written in Hebrew characters and with some Hebrew words mixed in. There was a flourishing Yiddish theater in New York City for a generation early in this century, with its own humor and pathos reflected directly in the long-running musical "Fiddler on the Roof," but indirectly reflected in the styles of entertainment that have become familiar to all Americans on stage and screen.

It is hard to determine whether Jewish culture has been Americanized or has itself deeply influenced American culture. America has furnished a hospitable setting for Jews, but it would be impossible to calculate just how much a part of this process was played by the attempt to adapt Judaism to the conditions of modern America. And if one tries to calculate the outcome of the religious intentions also present in the reorganization of the Conservative movement, the answer is probably not yet available. It seems clear that many Conservative leaders were unrealistically hopeful, early in the century, that a fairly adequate religious solution could be found by traditional means—that is, by a more liberal but still an Orthodox interpretation of the Torah, the authoritative first five books of the Old Testament, and of the rabbinic tradition based on them. The Reform way was of course impossible for the newer immigrants who wished to remain religious, but the problem has been to decide on what basis Conservative rabbis could make distinctions between rules that should be kept and those that could safely be dispensed with. For the Orthodox, of course, there was little distinction: All rules had to be obeyed because they were given by God. Any other position seemed a mere compromise for which any rationale was but a rationalization, an excuse for doing something wrong.

Nevertheless the Conservative movement was based on a soundly educated group of rabbis and congregations of men who at least respected the Jewish tradition. Since the focus of its attention was on credible reinterpretation of the ancient ways, the Conservative movement succeeded Reform as the means of expression for new possibilities of unconventional religious practice within Judaism. Thus in the thirties Mordecai Kaplan, a creative teacher at the Jewish Theological Seminary, began to implement a new approach to the question of a Jewish identity in the modern world by concluding that Judaism is not so much a religion, which entails a recognition of the authority of a revealed truth, as it is a civilization, which, like all civilizations, possesses a distinctive religious tradition, its own life-style.[7] The Jews should therefore stress the value of their cultural heritage for their own self-enrichment, rather than their uniqueness in the eyes of God or the particular religious beliefs distinguishing them from other people and thus isolating them socially. Kaplan's position was much discussed and gained considerable sympathy among many in Reform and Conservative circles. A journal, *The Reconstructionist,* was founded to communicate his point of view. But there was much hesitation among Kaplan and his followers about forming a movement around his position, which would then become a fourth, sectarian division; they preferred to see Jews united as a single people within the American system. It was therefore only in 1968 that a rabbinical training institution was founded, in Philadelphia.

Despite the fact that few Jews have made a formal commitment to a kind of Reconstructionist denomination within Judaism, it has been said that the Reconstructionist point of view is really that of most Jews in America. Its position is compatible with the ordinary assumptions made by most Americans about the place of religious institutions in their lives, and yet it tries to recover respect for some of the more important elements of the Jewish tradition. For Kaplan, unlike the leaders of the earlier Reform movement, the old rules and ceremonials of Judaism were too important to be brushed aside or reinterpreted in the direction of universal standards of rational morality. It is not that Kaplan believed them to be divinely given

7. Kaplan's major work on the Reconstructionist point of view is *Judaism as a Civilization* (New York: The Macmillan Company, 1935).

for all time, any more than the earlier Reform leaders did, but that he recognized their sociological importance for the community of Jews and their persistence as a distinct people. While Reform was uncomfortable with the hope for a reestablished holy nation in Palestine, Reconstructionists could welcome Israel as a Jewish state. The idea of the chosen people, particularly favored by God, was difficult for both groups to accept. In other words, people need effective ways of establishing their particular identity in a diverse world, but it is divisive to go beyond asking for recognition of their worth and to demand consideration for being better or more important than anyone else.

The Reconstructionist point of view gave considerable latitude for individuals in matters of observance. You were to do what fostered your identity as a Jew and could legitimately avoid what seemed to you to stand in the way of that end. The dietary laws, for example, have a communal and a disciplinary value, and they should be observed in a Jewish home for these reasons. Yet it is not reasonable to be observant in all circumstances, as the traditionally Orthodox are; for the Reconstructionist such rigid observance is to make a fetish of the law. Thus it is not inconsistent to eat the same food as others do in public, even though you keep a strictly kosher table at home. For the Reconstructionist there is no reason to deny himself the right to participate fully in American public life.

Another restrictive aspect of the tradition has been the separation of men and women in religious matters. Reconstructionism has taken a strong position in favor of the religious equality of men and women. Orthodox practice continues to insist that women be seated separately in the synagogue, that worship is a male prerogative. Indeed, the pious man gives thanks to God daily that he was not born a woman, without concern for secular developments that have put great pressure on such religious traditions. By contrast, the student body of the Reconstructionist rabbinical college includes a few women as potential candidates for the rabbinate, and synagogues associated with Reconstructionism, like those of Reform, insist on seating men and women together.

Thus Reconstructionism recommends itself as a movement that tries to find the most vital form of Judaism for people who want a faith compatible with modern scientific knowledge. As we have seen, its version of the tradition may be closer to what most American Jews believe than any other position in the spectrum of Judaism.

One might therefore have expected it to be an unconventional belief to which the majority of religious Jews would rally. But there is no sign that that has been or will be the case. Why should this be so? Perhaps Reconstructionism in retrospect will seem to have been a better response to the conditions of the twenties and thirties than to those of the postwar era. When Mordecai Kaplan began to teach, it seemed terribly important to formulate religious faith in ways that were consistent with the findings of modern science, which was seen then as the chief force for progress, whereas religion was often considered backward looking. Like many American thinkers of this century, Kaplan was impressed by the philosophy of John Dewey, by the pragmatic principle that what counted was not so much the idea in itself but its effect on people's lives. At this time Jews were less securely established in American life and more likely to be discriminated against. The better educated children of Orthodox immigrants were likely to find Reconstructionism an exciting interpretation of what they had been taught, much as contemporary Catholics discover undreamed-of riches in biblical criticism that liberal Protestants have long taken for granted and now tend to ignore. Reconstructionism also gave such Jews a good reason for observing their religion either privately or in their family life alone, with the result that their religious identity would involve fewer difficulties for their careers. They could be good Americans but also better Jews than the rationalists of Reform and Ethical Culture.

It may be that the advantages of Reconstructionism are seen as *only* practical. Would it not be plausible to conclude that Reconstructionism has not yet offered enough *religiously* to be a rallying point for strong Jewish loyalties? Like Reform, it was a set of ideas, a way of compromising the claims of tradition without abandoning the faith altogether, but it did not aggressively recruit rabbis and congregations to a sectarian banner. At the same time, it was too much a set of ideas about the value of using tradition for the sake of one's own spiritual betterment—and not enough an obligation that one *had* to honor and that encouraged deep feeling. It represented the traditional claims of Judaism more accurately than Reform did, but the individual could select from among them the ones that suited his own needs, with the result that community feeling was damaged when most needed. Will Herberg has written that among groups of recent immigrants there is a strong tendency for the third generation to try to rediscover its roots: "What the son wishes to forget, the grandson wishes to remember." Reconstructionism spoke to such a basic nostalgia, but nostalgia is not a very powerful motive in the long run. It is important to people who are basically comfortable with their existence. But people have become more anxious in recent times, more ready for radical answers, more willing to be enlisted for action, less detached and intellectual about questions that cannot really be answered but require the commitment of faith. Any religious institution that requires only conventional participation has lost credibility for many because institutions generally have begun to be perceived as inadequate to the needs for which they were originally intended. They neither control the people who need to be controlled nor inspire them with the faith they need to help them gain control of themselves.

THE NEW JEW AND UNCONVENTIONAL RELIGION

For Jews, recent history has posed questions about their religious self-awareness that are even more fundamental than those posed for Catholics by the Second Vatican Council and the changes it set in motion. Two critical developments have evoked agonies of reawakening and redefinition so profound that the questions of intellectual credibility that so engaged Isaac Mayer Wise and Mordecai Kaplan now seem secondary to questions about whether Judaism has any reason for being at all. One crisis has been the virulent anti-Semitism of recent times. Far from yielding to modern enlightenment, this feeling produced the holocaust of the Nazi years and, more recently, the continued discrimination against Jews who practice their faith in the Soviet Union. The other major event of modern times for Jews has been the establishment of Israel as a nation. Though generally a positive development, an answer to the yearnings of countless Jews for a haven from oppression and fear, Israel has at some points sharpened the question of what a Jewish identity means in the modern world. The depth of feeling produced by these related events has also sharpened the criticism of traditional Judaism by those who are Jewish by birth, and indirectly it has ensured that the unconventional Judaism of contemporary times will move much further from traditional forms than the movements we have described thus far.

Why is this the case? One reason may be that, as we have already noted, Judaism has presented itself to its people so much more in terms of standards of behavior than as a matter of faith, by contrast to Christianity. If this is true, and if it is also true that today is a time when people are calling for a greater depth of feeling in religion, one would expect the unconventional impulse in Judaism to be expressed in groups that provide experience rather than new ways to alter traditional practice or rethink the old faith. One may guess that it is less satisfactory to contemporary Jews than it was to their forbears to discover that they are a people defined by their religious tradition, unless that discovery enables them to live the experience deeply, not just reflect about it.

The problem is posed with particular force by the brute fact of the holocaust, the virtual destruction of everything Jewish in the areas controlled by the Axis powers in Europe during the Second World War.[8] It is not only that every Jew was threatened with death in those days, so that mere survival was a miracle, but that the murder of so many people for no reason except their lineage made no sense in religious terms. From the days of ancient Israel, the tradition had turned adversity to some use by making it the occasion to lament the people's failure to serve God as He required. Evil might make no sense in the life of a single Jew, but it could be compensated for by the thought of the importance of Israel as a holy people. They might suffer for a time, but ultimately they would be vindicated.

In the light of recent events many Jews have felt that they could not possibly find the same kind of meaning in the Nazi slaughter. To state it bluntly, if God really rules the world, no sinfulness imaginable justifies that punishment. And if He does not rule, then He is not God. There is a militant minority among Jews that has organized self-defense groups and vowed "Never again" to Jews suffering injury without striking back. Similarly, there is a kind of theological "Never again," which asks how anything like the traditional Judaism is even thinkable in the aftermath of the wanton destruction of so many. One result is that some Jews have repudiated their faith altogether, but others have called for an end to assimilation in order not to compromise Judaism and make Jews like everyone else. These "new Jews" intend to work out a more genuinely religious Judaism, a seriously committed community that no longer worries so much about what its neighbors among other faiths will think. There is a militancy among Jews just as there is among numbers of other groups that previously kept their sufferings to themselves.

How much of this ardor will take a religious direction and what form will it take? We shall look presently at a few groups that show what is happening with some unconventional believers among Jews, but before doing so we must say a word about the other fact that has profoundly influenced how all Jews think about their religious tradition, namely the State of Israel. Before its founding in 1948, Israel was the "impossible dream" of many Jews, the goal of their

8. See, for example, Richard L. Rubenstein, "Job and Auschwitz," in Marty and Peerman, eds., *New Theology* (New York: The Macmillan Company, 1971), Vol. 8, pp. 270–90.

aspiration to be restored as a chosen people in a holy land. Since coming into being, Israel has made a home for displaced Jews from everywhere, but it has done so in ways that could not possibly satisfy everyone. Those particularly upset are the Jews for whom Israel was a religious dream. There is a religious party in Israel, but it is a distinct minority and largely a curiosity to most Israelis, who are rational and practical in politics and more likely to be socialist than anything else. In religious terms the pious minority is narrowly Orthodox, and its members do not engage in anxious questioning about their identity, in contrast to American Jews. In Israel most people are too busy to worry about such things. It is a small and beleaguered country busily occupied with resettling its immigrants. Often Judaism is seen as an obstacle to this work. Issues that arise have to do with the legal definition of who is a Jew, or questions of observance of the sabbath—points about which the religious law is unequivocal. Except on very public and traditional issues, religious opinion is not taken very seriously by Israeli leaders and policy makers.

Nevertheless, the existence of Israel makes an important point for any religious Jew. He may always go there, if he wishes, and he can no longer take refuge in a hope that once seemed impossible to fulfill. No longer may a Jew mourn the nation condemned to enforced exile. To stay in America, to live out his life as an American Jew, is a choice and not a matter of destiny. Jews can no longer make easy excuses to themselves for accepting a kind of second-rate religion, a compromised faith. On the other hand, since Israel is not nearly so much the religious nation many had hoped it would be, the hope itself has to be transmuted into something else.

Thus Jewishness in the modern world begins to appear not what it used to be—an identity that was the product of a particular historical fate—but something more positive, a spiritual heritage that can be affirmed openly as a value for other people as well.[9] But in the religious sense it can easily be nothing at all to be a Jew—only citizenship in an aggressive, thoroughly pragmatic, modern nation, if one is an Israeli, or successful participation in business or professional life in a liberal urban setting in America or elsewhere. In the latter case Jewish identity ceases to be very relevant, though it may generate a conventional membership and occasional routine participation in the affairs of a subgroup of the population. In particular, it has often involved some participation in the prodigious

9. See the discussion on Jewishness and Judaism in Nathan Glazer, *American Judaism* (Chicago: University of Chicago Press, 1957).

efforts devoted to the raising of funds for characteristic purposes—hospitals and other charitable institutions, educational establishments for both religious and secular learning, and above all, the Israeli nation-building effort.

In the light of these recent decisive events, some Jews believe that the truly Jewish identity for the modern age calls for forms of commitment that by previous standards seem extreme, even bizarre. For years, many people who were ethnically Jewish but convinced that their religious tradition was bankrupt have vigorously supported secular causes—the labor movement, liberal and radical politics, social work, the mental health movement. It is significant that what may be the two most influential ways of analyzing modern human experience—Marxism and psychoanalysis—were the work of Jewish intellectuals who had rejected their religious tradition. Those intellectual options are still open, but for a variety of reasons they have disappointed many who once put high hopes in them. For one thing, Jews still suffer in the Soviet Union, the home of the Marxist revolution. Such facts dictate a rejection of the way of accommodation that so many Jews have followed in trying to adjust their ancient tradition to modern times.

Why then should not Jews give up halfway measures, reverse the familiar trends of modern times, and become more openly Jewish? That they should change direction is a major implication of the phrase "Never again." The response is a variety of groups that are enlisting the unconventional believers among Jews today. Though the expressions are diverse, the common feature of these movements is a kind of militant Jewishness, even when the focus is ethnic identity rather than religious commitment. The Jewish Defense League, a group gathered around a rabbi named Meir Kahane, is one such ethnic response. Founded in 1968, members of this group first became conspicuous by organizing roving anticrime patrols in sections of Brooklyn in which Jewish people were being mugged and robbed. The league was not liked by the police, who often find anything resembling a citizen's army to be an invitation to violence; but the group gained widespread publicity, which helped change the image of the Jew as a passive victim. In more recent years the league has expanded its activities to include agitation in favor of the rights of Jews in the Soviet Union, especially their right to emigrate to Israel.[10] Rabbi Kahane has divided his time between Israel and America, and he has aroused dislike as well as ardent support in

10. Articles on the Jewish Defense League appeared in several New York publications in the early 1970's.

both countries. But the Jewish Defense League has little claim to being distinctive in a religious sense, and as such it is not that relevant to our study of unconventional believers among Jews.

HASIDISM

If we look elsewhere, however, we can find examples of unconventional Jewish groups that fulfill the image we have used previously of growth at the edges, where conventional Judaism meets its strict Orthodox past on the one hand, and where, on the other, a newly radical Judaism forms groups seemingly unlike anything seen before in the Jewish past. Their common element is intensity of commitment. On the side of tradition, a conspicuous development in contemporary times has been the proliferation of ardently pious groups associated with people called Hasidim. The origins of this movement go back as far as the pre-Christian era. That is, Hasidism inherits the traditions of many groups of Jews who did not regard mainstream Judaism as sufficient for their religious needs. If mainstream Judaism was based on learned interpretation of the law and strict observance of the *mitzvot*, the Judaism of the Hasidim was based on finding ways to approach God more directly, either through an ever stricter piety or through a mystical experience cultivated in special ways of reading the Scriptures, or through a combination of both. Judaism is an elitist faith in many ways, and traditional Judaism is an elitism of learning. Hasidism, in the happy phrase of one of its interpreters, is an "open elite" in that it is accessible to the unlearned who are sufficiently pious.

The Hasidism of more modern times dates from the beginning of the eighteenth century with the career of a Polish Jew named Israel ben Eliezer, who came to be known as the Baal Shem Tov, the "master of the good name," meaning the holy name of God.[11] The movement began in the wake of one of the several great bursts of anti-Semitic persecution that have disfigured relations between Jewish and Christian communities. This had taken place in the middle of the seventeenth century and had been followed by the appearance of a man whom many Jews believed was the long-awaited Messiah. He proved false, but there was still a need for the kind of emotional support that many felt was missing in the tradition of orthodoxy. Part of the reason for this feeling was that Jewish

11. Martin Buber wrote several books on Hasidism, including *The Origin and Meaning of Hasidism* (New York: Horizon Press, Inc., 1960).

communities decimated by murderous pogroms had lost the freedom to govern themselves or had seen that freedom sharply curtailed, so that the status of rabbis as judges of disputes within the communities was compromised. But more important were the unsatisfied religious needs of many Jews of that time. The Baal Shem Tov, at any rate, is remembered through a multitude of semilegendary stories that portray him as a humble man who taught others by means of his intense piety rather than by his doctrine. He was certainly not indifferent to the learned tradition, nor was he unconcerned with the religious discipline of prayer. But what mattered most to him was love of God and the cultivation of an ecstatic spirit of devotion that alone rendered prayer authentic.

Hasidism to this day retains the essential features of the legacy of the Baal Shem Tov.[12] It consists of groups of pious Jews united around rabbis noted for their religiosity as well as their learning. The groups are named after the towns in Eastern Europe in which the founders originally gathered their following. As one example, a group now located in Brooklyn, where a number of Hasidic communities flourish, was founded in the White Russian town of Lubavitch; its leader, whatever his name, is known as the Lubavitcher Rebbe. Sometimes the leadership is inherited, but the rebbe of each group must be capable of inspiring piety in his followers. On the other hand, in the days since the Baal Shem Tov much of the hostility between rabbinic orthodoxy and Hasidism has disappeared, with the result that Hasidic groups outdo the merely orthodox in devotion to observance of *mitzvot* and to traditional learning, as well as in the fervor of their worship.

What is life like in a Hasidic community? First of all, it turns your attention from involvement in everyday interests to devotion to the concerns of the group. In America this means resistance to the modernization and adaptation so characteristic of other forms of Judaism. The drawing of boundaries between the Hasidim and outsiders has not been accomplished by retreating to the country, after the fashion of the Amish, the Hutterites, or other Christian sects, but the effect is quite similar. The Hasidim are geographically isolated in a way, since there are sections of Brooklyn that they have practically made their own. But they are also set apart by a distinctive style of dress and appearance, particularly the men.

12. Arthur A. Cohen edited a book entitled *A People Apart* (New York: E. P. Dutton & Co., Inc., 1970), with many sensitive photographs of contemporary Hasidim by Philip Garvin. For information on sociological aspects of the movement, see Solomon Poll, *The Hasidic Community of Williamsburg* (Glencoe, Ill.: The Free Press, 1962).

The role of women in Hasidism is defined in very traditional ways. They marry, preside over the home, and provide their husbands with as many healthy children as family circumstances permit. They also pray, but as in Orthodox practice they are segregated or even screened from acts of corporate worship outside the home, and they do not participate in the periodic *farbrengen* meetings, when the men congregate to hear discourses by the rebbe and to celebrate their oneness in their devotion to God, the Holy One. When Hasidic women marry, their husbands are chosen for them, they shave their heads as a check against being too seductive and cover them with wigs, and they even celebrate with the other women while the men toast the bridegroom's new status. It is not a liberated role, to say the least, but certainly not without its dignity. In everyday life Hasidic women dress like sober, industrious, respectable matrons, which is what they are content to be.

The men, by contrast, cannot be mistaken for men of other faiths. They are bearded, and long locks of hair hang from their temples. The head is always covered, either by the old medieval monk's skullcap, called a *yarmulke,* or by a conventional black hat. Soberly dressed for everyday occasions—usually in black suit, white shirt, and dark tie—on any day except the Sabbath they work at occupations which do not seem at variance with the canons of their faith. Whenever the occasion offers, they devote themselves to prayer and study of the Torah. They make their living when possible within the Hasidic community, selling kosher food and other religious articles or performing services necessary within the community. Otherwise they make as good a living as they can outside, though always in morally justifiable work and always with regard to the priority of their religious obligations.

What has been said thus far would be unlikely to attract anyone to Hasidism and certainly would not explain why in contemporary times the Hasidic groups have been able not only to preserve themselves through a conspicuously higher birth rate than is normal for the American Jewish population, but even to attract new members, particularly from among educated young Jews. How, then, is this attraction of new numbers to be explained? The rigor of their religious life may be attractive to those who find conventional Jewish piety unrewarding. But probably of more importance is the vitality and exuberance of religious celebrations of the Hasidim. One such occasion is the annual holiday of Simhath Torah, which comes in the fall and celebrates the gift of the Torah. The particular occasion is the end of the yearly cycle of liturgical reading and the start of a new round. It is a happy day in Orthodox circles, since it provides an opportunity to give thanks for the supreme gift, the Torah, a name which means Law and study but also refers to the scrolls on which the texts are written. Such scrolls are an essential element for the conduct of ritual. They are never destroyed; in worship they are reverently brought out of their repository, unrolled to the portion appropriate for the day, and as carefully returned until the next Sabbath.

On Simhath Torah the scroll becomes a bride; the scroll ends are decked in silver ornaments while richly embroidered covers protect the parchments themselves. After prayers the scroll is snatched up and a dancing procession forms, circling the synagogue to the lively singing of a psalm that tells how the Lord, as King of His people, leads them to eternal victory. The celebration goes on for hours, boys and men singing and dancing in company, while in some small synagogues the girls and women listen and watch from behind makeshift barriers. Outside it is apparent that holiday is all around. Jews less caught up in their faith take the opportunity to visit and observe these enclaves. Police barricades keep out traffic, and crowds of people stroll in the streets from synagogue to synagogue. Groups of teenagers use the occasion to congregate with each other, and everyone is happy.

In the Hasidic areas the distinctiveness of their practice is readily apparent on such a day. The men put on holiday dress, wide-brimmed fur hats, knickers, and long coats. Each item in this costume must be earned by communal awareness of the depth of the individual's piety. Historically, this clothing originated in the styles worn by the Polish nobility and by well-to-do Jews in the days before the pogroms. But like the robes of Christian priests, which originated in the upper-class dress of Roman times, such costumes have become the marks of spiritual rank, which can be earned and are proudly displayed. In one Hasidic center a large crowd of men gathers for one of the *farbrengen* occasions of the year. The rebbe gives an extended discourse. The intensity of attention is too great to be prolonged as one session, so while the rebbe retires to recover his strength the men wait in good spirits, passing around little cups of whiskey and discussing what has been said. No such theological participation is conceivable in Christian circles, except perhaps in some of the Germanic groups like the Dutch Reformed and the Mennonites. Such participation is unconventional from the point of view of Christianity as well as that of most American Jews.

Why, then, has Hasidism found new life in this country in recent years? And will it continue to thrive here? A number of special circumstances make these questions hard to answer. These individual groups depend on remarkable leadership, and one cannot predict whether enough men of sufficient stature will appear out of American Judaism to carry on the traditions of Hasidism. It is apparent, for example, that much of the vitality of the current movement is a response to the enormous impact of the Nazi experience on surviving Jews, much as the response to the Baal Shem Tov seems to have been strengthened by seventeenth-century pogroms. The current leaders are European refugees, and many of the most ardent followers of the rebbes are survivors of decimated families who find in Hasidic groups the replacement for their lost kinsmen. It also remains an open question whether the high birth rate of the Hasidim and their strong community bonds will suffice for the provision of new members and the continued loyalty of the old. One might also wonder whether the urban situation in America in years to come will appear so hazardous that Hasidic groups will wish to move elsewhere. At least one group has emigrated from America to Israel, which will probably continue to offer a haven to the Jews of the world.

On the other hand, ethnic identities have been reasserted in America in recent years, and to be traditionally Jewish is no longer so alien here once one finds a community of like-minded people. These groups are small compared with the total number of Jews in the country, but only a few young people disillusioned with conventional Jewish ways are needed to make up the necessary numbers, if suitable leaders are available. Since the level of education of Jews in America is now far higher than it was before World War II, it is possible to foresee that there will be significant numbers of young Jews who will be attracted by the unique Hasidic combination of devotion to the traditional intellectual pursuits of Judaism and joyful commitment to a fully ritualized daily existence.

RADICAL GROUPS

To the extent that recruitment of young people alienated from conventional Judaism is a key to predicting the future of Hasidism in America, we must determine whether there is significant evidence that such alienation is finding other religious forms of expression. Two movements may be briefly mentioned whose status is in doubt because they involve very few younger Jews and because they have not achieved the stability of the Hasidic movement. We have in mind those more radical movements that attempt to find new forms of communal life that will be Jewish without succumbing to the institutionalism of the synagogue.[13]

One such movement is radical in social form but traditionalist in religious practice. Much as Christian groups seek to reproduce the conditions of the earliest followers of what was called the way before there was a Christian church, so groups of Jews have gathered together in what are called *havurot*. These are groups based on the idea that authentic congregational worship is impossible without communal living. Consequently they are located in houses large enough to accommodate a fair number of people. They are found in urban settings, particularly Boston and New York City, where it is easy to obtain food that does not violate Jewish dietary laws. The communal living lends greater significance to eating together in obedience to Jewish law than is the case in the family experience of most Jews in contemporary America, and certainly worship means more. The aim of each such group is to have in residence a kind of natural *minyan*, founded on the basis of a degree of sincerity, an intensity of intimacy not discovered elsewhere. The appeal of such groups is obvious, especially since they do not require meticulous obedience to all legal requirements of Judaism, but in some ways their strength is in practice a source of considerable difficulty. Most of the membership has been drawn from university communities, people who in many cases are not year-round residents of the communities in which the *havurot* are situated. More significantly, the desire to live on closer and more spiritually intimate terms with others is not always the same as willingness to share oneself with others on such levels. Interviews with members of one of the best-known such groups showed that what might be called the problem of self-consciousness had not been fully resolved and probably would not be resolved, at least not nearly so effectively as it seems to have been by Hasidic groups.

By contrast, a *havurah*-like group based in Washington, D. C., has tried to confront in a different way the problem of the seeming irrelevance of traditionally Jewish patterns of living. Just as many disenchanted liberals among groups of Protestant or Catholic background have determined that it is the will of God for contemporary people to become activists in great social issues—such as civil rights and more recently the prolonged war in Vietnam—so these few Jews have tried to express their faith in a new way. For them the Hasidic

13. See *The New Jews*, edited by James A. Sleeper and Alan L. Mintz (New York: Vintage Books, 1971), and Jacob Neusner, ed., *Contemporary Judaic Fellowship in Theory and in Practice* (New York: Ktav Publishing House, Inc., 1972).

version of Judaism is a kind of museum piece, and the other *havurot* are not courageous enough to avoid being regarded as merely new ways of adapting to American culture to avoid being overwhelmed by the Christian majority. Thus in the name of justice—the same prophetic theme that has helped fuel Christian efforts out of the legacy of the Old Testament—this group joined the great antiwar demonstrations in Washington, D. C., as worshiping Jews, wearing their prayer shawls and violating curfews to say their service on the steps of public buildings.

A central figure in this effort is a man named Arthur Waskow, an activist learned enough to translate this effort into a new liturgy. In a work called *The Freedom Seder* he has taken the old family ritual for Passover—a celebration of the mighty work of the Lord in delivering Israel from slavery in Egypt—and reworked it into a universal appeal for the end of all oppression.[14] Since the traditional seder includes confession and affirmation of the need for a new beginning, Waskow's seder calls on Jews to confess their complicity in the existing system and to demand radical change. It is a work of considerable imagination, and it is sufficiently relevant to the tradition to provide any Jew who takes his religion seriously with some discomfort.

This acute novelty is at the same time the chief weakness of such a movement. It runs too directly contrary to what most Jews feel is their major task: trying to discover the meaning of being a Jew in a culture that expresses a colossal indifference to their apartness. Waskow asks, in effect, that one become first a serious Jew and then transform his faith again and engage it actively within the same society from which his Judaism has effectively separated him. Few Jews are likely to find it possible to bend their lives into such a pattern; more importantly, Waskow's message seems unlikely to appeal to many Jews as a valid religious alternative, since in recent times their political radicalism has been of an unreligious nature, and their religious radicalism, as we have seen, an intensification of commitment to traditional Judaism. It seems most likely that for Jews the alternatives of conventional and unconventional belief will continue to be set before them in the more familiar ways, the choice between the synagogues of settled Jewish communities and the more demanding religiosity of something like Hasidism.

14. Arthur Waskow published *The Freedom Seder* (New York: Holt, Rinehart and Winston, 1969).

The Unconventional
in the Denominations

As we have seen, the outsider's image of a homogeneous Catholicism is a distortion of a situation of considerable diversity. Similarly, there are three major divisions of Judaism, but there are also several other religious or quasi-religious possibilities for Jews. Even the three traditional divisions among Jews have occasioned much controversy and ill feeling within the Jewish community.

How much worse, therefore, is the application of a single term, "Protestant," to the host of religious groups ranging from the fundamentalist to the Unitarian in doctrine, or in worship from the Quaker meeting to the Latin Mass of some Episcopal churches. It is true that most Protestants are gathered into a relatively few denominational groups, and that many of these "families" are quite closely related historically, but the remaining differences are by no means unimportant. Thus what is conventional belief and practice from the viewpoint of one tradition may look very unconventional to others; it may therefore seem virtually impossible to establish with any clarity what the unconventional is for Protestant denominations. Moreover, the Protestant communities in their variety have offered far more scope for the expression of unconventional belief than have the other, more ancient traditions. Indeed, the term "Protestant" may be so inexact just because it is applied to any group considered unconventional by reference to Catholicism during recent centuries.

In the past, many Protestant groups established themselves as unconventional believers in America by forsaking a traditional spiritual home and seeking another.[1] Such was, after all, the motivation of the Pilgrims, the Puritans, and many other early settlers of the New World. The New Englanders were unconventional believers from the Church of England. One of their constant anxieties during the Colonial period concerned what they would do if the government in London tried to assign them a bishop and impose on them the religious discipline required of English subjects. Roger Williams, who formed a settlement for Baptists in Rhode Island, and William Penn, who wanted to experiment with religious toleration, are other prominent examples of men who wanted to found institutions for unconventional religious expression.

Even George Calvert, Baron Baltimore, the Catholic lord whose son realized his father's hope of becoming proprietor of the colony of Maryland, was expressing a distinctly unconventional intention by English standards, for ever since the beginning of the reign of Queen Elizabeth I, in the middle of the sixteenth century, practicing Catholics in England had risked civil penalties and mortal danger. Since the colonists were all subjects of the British Crown, it proved difficult to establish even this small haven for Catholics. Outnumbered by Protestants who harbored all the traditional English prejudices against them, they soon found themselves subject to anti-Catholic discrimination for a time, even in their own colony.

In other words, from the English point of view the unconventional in religious belief and practice was the rule rather than the exception in many of the American colonies. Curiously enough, however, often those who were unconventional in their definition of the faith were quite conventional in believing that there should be a single church for all members of the community, and that those who were in disagreement could not remain within it. Thus the New England Puritans attempted to establish on Massachusetts Bay a "better" Church of England. This establishment survived the Revolutionary War and was not finally abolished until 1833. Many good churchmen saw no reason to prohibit such establishments when the colonies became states. They felt it inconsistent to allow the expression of alternative religious beliefs, since unity was for them a religious as well as a political ideal. Religious dissenters were welcome to go to Rhode Island or Pennsylvania and be literally

1. Of many available introductions to the history of religion in America, particularly Protestantism, perhaps the most accessible is Winthrop S. Hudson's *Religion in America*, 2d ed. (New York: Charles Scribner's Sons, Inc., 1973). See also Martin E. Marty, *Righteous Empire* (New York: The Dial Press, 1970).

damned because of their opposition to the religion of the majority. Thus the attitudes that fostered suppression of unconventional religion long outlived the revolution.

Clearly, however, it was a practical impossibility to legislate a single religious establishment for the republic, whose member states already represented several diverse religious traditions. Thus those who favored an established religion had to accept the notion of those Virginia gentlemen like Jefferson who held the novel idea that freedom of choice in matters of faith was a positive good. In that time of competing religious loyalties, no single faith could be given preference. Ultimately the competition tended to confirm the principle of choice as preferable to the principle of coercion. In other words, not only did the Bill of Rights clearly foreshadow the end of established religion, but it also created the possibility for new groups to gain legitimacy on the same basis as the old ones. Originally this was chiefly a legal right, but it soon became a pervasive social reality. The groups that flourished and became influential in a measure impossible for the older churches were the ones that directed their efforts to gaining the voluntary support of people whom they treated as free individuals, who could choose to be saved by admitting their sins and repenting. Historically speaking, therefore, the religious initiative in American Protestantism passed to the unconventional believer with the founding of a national government without a national church. Next we examine what happened to that initiative in succeeding years.

THE RELIGION OF THE REPUBLIC

In the early years of the American republic, there were more Congregational churches than any other kind, the legacy of the Puritans still being valued even if the churches they had founded had considerably changed in spirit. Despite its continued importance, the Congregational denomination and other traditional colonial churches were not in a position to grow as rapidly as the nation. The Church of England, once second in importance, grew much less rapidly in a time when loyalty to England was a disability. It was some time, in fact, before its new identity, the Protestant Episcopal Church, commended itself to Americans. Even by the end of the revolution, two other groups had outstripped in membership the English national church in this country. These were the Presbyterians and the Baptists. By the beginning of the nineteenth century there were probably more Baptists than members of any other denomination. The Methodists, who were to provide the most dynamic example of Protestant growth during the new century, had only just been established here at the end of the eighteenth.

Already to a well-informed observer it might have been apparent that the future of Protestantism belonged to groups of a distinctly unconventional character. The similarity of all these groups only underscores the validity of this judgment. All of them were of British origin, in the first place. Scotsmen had a Presbyterian national church but no establishment on this side of the water. Among Englishmen the Presbyterians were a minority, but their faith was close enough to that of the Puritans to make it possible for Congregationalists and Presbyterians to cooperate in evangelizing the West, where they had to compete with the sometimes poorly educated but ardent Baptists, Methodists, and Quakers. In such circumstances, traditional religious views made little sense, and a settled church organization of the older sort was impossible.

Methodism managed to live uneasily with its Church of England obligations in the home country and to dispense with them in the New World. This was the case especially after the revolution ended hope of adding to the small number of Anglican clergy of Methodist persuasion who had emigrated here. In this emergency Wesley stood on his authority as a presbyter of the Church of England to ordain the men who would be called bishops in the Methodist denomination in America, arguing that there was no essential scriptural difference between the two church offices. The result was that the Methodist church in America could train leaders adapted to its own needs and not inhibited by traditional restrictions. Thus it became the most effective evangelizing force of the first half of the nineteenth century and the constant competitor with the Baptists for numerical leadership among the Protestant denominations.

The Baptists in turn were groups of believers who had much in common with the New England Puritans but who initially made themselves conspicuous (or notorious), by coming to two related decisions. These decisions were of great significance not only for the way in which the Baptists understood themselves and were understood by others; they were also significant for the effect that their growth had on American Protestant thinking about the proper place of religious institutions in society. The Baptists, like the Puritans generally, thought it scandalous that churches should include anyone who was not a convinced believer, what used to be called a "proven saint." The first of the two decisions was to restore believers' —that is, adult—baptism as a mark of regeneration and death of sin, in accordance with the New Testament. Probably taking their cue from the Anabaptists (or "rebaptizers"), who had suffered so much persecution on the Continent, English Baptists rejected infant baptism and instituted the practice of immersion only of people old enough to understand the faith and experience true repentance. They also applied the logic of this practice to the view that no government could coerce people into faith, and that therefore churches should be separate from the state and organized on a voluntary basis.

In addition, Baptists were pioneers in holding to a belief in religious liberty on a religious basis, rather than on the basis of the faith in reason which was to animate men like Thomas Jefferson. For Baptists, each church was an entity unto itself, although it might associate with others for mutual support. The sovereignty of the individual conscience, as ruled by God through revelation in the Scriptures, was in turn the basis for the associations that constituted each individual church. Baptists consider themselves to be under divine, not human, authority, and it follows that churches should not be under governmental authority, since that too is human. Thus Baptist churches are not small monarchies ruled by men whose ordination sets them apart and above criticism, and who in *their* turn are subordinate to higher authorities in a chain of command. Baptist clergy are preachers, primarily, rather than celebrators of the Eucharist, as Catholic priests have been. And as preachers, their leaders are expected to manifest spiritual qualities rather than learning. Thus although Baptists maintain a strong if generally conservative educational system for prospective ministers, many a spiritually inspired layman in former times was able to establish a congregation on the basis of some knowledge of the Bible and the ability to impart that knowledge to his people. No one from the outside could overrule him because the congregation was his judge. And from the start there was a strong tendency to identify inspiration with the power to speak movingly.

The Methodists succeeded by devising an organization to bring religion to people who were not being reached by traditional religious forms, either physically, on the frontier, or spiritually, in the more sedate settled churches of the coastal areas. The Baptists varied the procedure by renouncing all but local structures for the sake of realizing in communities the latent readiness to respond to a simple but sensible and moving version of the faith in personal redemption that could be read out of the Bible. A significant adjunct to the power of these evangelical efforts was provided by the use of genuinely popular music, hymns that effectively delivered the same message as the preacher but with the participation of the congregation as well.

All the churches of what came to be called the "evangelical" persuasion found it increasingly attractive to adopt some or all of these popular methods. Not incidentally, they were practices that had a strong affinity to American political forms as well, with the result that the evangelical church became for many Americans a training ground for citizenship. Over the years the methods that proved successful in converting large numbers of people came to be developed as the self-conscious technique of the "revival." Its dynamics began to be understood in the so-called Great Awakening of the 1740s; they were perfected in what the great revivalist Charles G. Finney called "new measures" a century later; and they have come to be "broadcast" by modern communications techniques in the hands of Billy Graham, Oral Roberts, and a host of others.[2]

CONVENTIONAL AND UNCONVENTIONAL PROTESTANTISM

Now it appears why the distinction between conventional and unconventional religion is so difficult to apply to the various Protestant traditions, and yet is so important for understanding them. Put as concisely as possible, the forms of the church and the methods of "winning souls"—that began as a response to a widely felt need for unconventional religious expression in a period dominated by traditional ones—became the conventional forms of succeeding times, when the churches they built up stood side by side with the surviving churches of the older denominations. In a frequently quoted passage, John Wesley predicted that because of their disciplined behavior his Methodist followers would tend to grow rich; he advised them therefore to become even richer in a spiritual sense by giving away all they could.[3] Needless to say, not all Methodists followed his advice, and so became comfortable, middle-class, and less zealous in the pursuit of perfection than their predecessors had been.

Similarly, believers' baptism could easily become not a sign of the reception of true grace but merely the mark of initiation into

2. William McLoughlin has edited Finney's *Lectures on Revivals of Religion* (Cambridge: Harvard University Press, 1960).

3. The text originated in the second volume of Southey's *Life of Wesley* and is quoted by Max Weber in *The Protestant Ethic and the Spirit of Capitalism* (New York: Charles Scribner's Sons, 1958), pp. 175–76, and by H. Richard Niebuhr in *The Social Sources of Denominationalism* (New York: Meridian Books, Inc., 1957), pp. 70–71.

another Christian denomination that could be considered by other Christians a harmonious part of the religious landscape. Thus the unconventional group could become the training ground for conventional believers as thoroughly as any older church could.

On the other hand, the strength of these forms and methods was the continued vitality they were able to generate in the evangelical churches; their best testimonial was that newer sectarian groups continued to be formed, in a spirit of disillusionment with the new conventionality of evangelical churches but out of the same materials. On occasion, of course, there was a new theological twist like the belief in the seventh day of the week as the proper day for worship—that is, Saturday instead of Sunday—or a fervent expectation of the swift return of Christ to judge the world, as with the Adventist groups or Jehovah's Witnesses. Thus there were many Baptist or quasi-Baptist groups formed during the nineteenth century. Although by no means all groups fell under strictly Baptist forms, it was a very rare group that lacked all features of the typical Baptist congregation, because that form of church organization suited so very well the conditions of the American environment.

The historian Sidney Mead has written that denominational Protestantism was shaped by historylessness, voluntaryism, the mission enterprise, revivalism, the flight from "reason," the triumph of pietism, and finally the competition between denominations.[4] Reduced to essentials, these descriptive characteristics add up to the image of religious groups recruited by appeals to present feelings, not past traditions, and maintained by the efforts of ordinary people to make their churches prosper in their own communities and to act in turn to spread the truth they know to others. This description fits the Baptist churches more than those of any other of the old denominations, which means that to be like the Baptists in important respects is a significant mark of many if not most of the American religious groups with unconventional beginnings.

In other words, what began as unconventional in America became commonplace, if not conventional, by traditional standards, and religious customs that originated as acts of principle often ended by being a familiar feature of the American religious scene. Thus to gather by the river for baptism comes to be a folk custom of the rural South, a by no means unusual aspect of the behavior of local, solid citizens. It is a far cry from the days when churchmen of the New York colony thought of the Rhode Island where Roger Wil-

4. Sidney Mead, *The Lively Experiment* (New York: Harper and Row, Publishers, Inc., 1963).

liams established his Baptist church as "the sewer of New England." [5] So when it became the accepted thing, especially in the South, to be either a Baptist or a Methodist (and a rare thing to be anything else), the role of the unconventional religious group had to change. Opportunities to express the unconventional impulse passed to the groups that offered the restless believer a chance to worship and be blessed in a deeper, or at least different, way than Baptists or Methodists offered.

Another factor complicating our understanding of the Protestant situation is the considerable regional difference where religion is concerned. [6] It is not just that the other major faiths are not equally distributed. The Catholic population in America is predominantly urban and suburban, but particularly strong in New England and in such cities as New York, St. Louis, other major urban areas of the upper Midwest, the old Louisiana territory at the mouth of the Mississippi, and in the southwestern Spanish mission territories. The Jewish group is much smaller but highly concentrated and therefore a strong voice especially in New York City, where about half the Jews of America live. It is also significant that the Protestant denominations are unevenly distributed. The most heavily Protestant area of the country is the southeast, the states of the old Confederacy, a significant fact since its churches are not only Protestant but in many cases belong to groups that separated from their northern counterparts well before the Civil War. The South is not only relatively poor and rural, but its conventional Protestantism is primarily Southern Baptist or Methodist. Therefore its unconventional religion will look different from what we meet elsewhere.

In other regions of the country the religious picture is very different. About two out of every three Americans belong to one of the Protestant denominations, but in New York City Protestants are in a minority, greatly outnumbered by Catholics and Jews and perhaps even by those of no religious affiliation. New York is in many ways unique but in no respect more so than in the distinctiveness of its population groups. In other cities Protestants are less likely to be outnumbered and in suburban areas have greatly predominated, as we noted in the first chapter. But whereas the South is largely Baptist or Methodist, in the Midwest and north central states the Protestant is likely to be a Lutheran and thus much more a tradi-

5. This phrase is quoted in Edwin Scott Gaustad, *Historical Atlas of Religion in America* (New York: Harper and Row, Publishers, 1962), p. 1. This work is a source for much of the historical material below.

6. *Ibid.,* p. 1.

tionalist than the Protestant of the South. In Utah and nearby parts of surrounding states, as we have seen, almost everyone is a Mormon. In the states of the northwest, unlike other regions of the country, no single religious group predominates. No single form of unconventional belief can therefore be found in all these regions, naturally.

On the other hand, people do speak of "mainline" Protestantism, and it does make sense to do so. The term refers to the older denominations taken collectively—the Methodists, or at least many of them; the northern or American Baptists, Lutherans, Presbyterians, Episcopalians, and Congregationalists. These denominations are distributed all over the country, and their members are generally middle-class people, reasonably well educated. This group of church members has been the target of countless barbs from liberal theologians, and of the reproaches of its more sensitive young people, directed at an apparent complacency and a too obvious or too pervasive conventionalism. In the Roman Catholic Church the usual target would be the bishops, the hierarchy, and the obedient but unthinking faithful, whereas in Judaism the entire synagogue or Reform temple establishment, together with the network of traditional fund-raising and social-service agencies, is looked at with disfavor by both sceptics and unconventional believers. In each case the unconventional response can take a number of forms, as we have demonstrated in previous chapters, and in the Protestant case this diversity has resulted in wholly new groups, some of which have been described in Part I.

Does this mean that there is no place for unconventional believers within the mainline or conventional Protestant groups? Not at all, though it would be an interesting but difficult question whether the structure of mainline Protestantism today makes unconventional expressions easier or more difficult than is the case with other faiths. We shall make some speculations on this point in the concluding chapter. For the moment, it is more important to show that there are many examples within the mainline groups of the possibility of going further than the ordinary boundaries of conventional religiosity.

A PARISH IN THE INNER CITY

When one begins to look seriously for unconventional responses within conventional Protestantism, the field of possibilities quickly becomes too thick with examples to represent adequately. It is not just a matter of the Southern Baptist or Methodist who joins a Holiness church or a stricter sectarian Baptist group or even becomes an Episcopalian or migrates to California and becomes a Congregationalist. Where the normal thing to do is to grow up and become an adult member of the same church your parents belong to, or to join a church of the same or a similar denomination in a suburban development not very different from the one in which you grew up, there are still many possibilities to go beyond what is offered by the conventions of Sunday worship and church fellowship activities.

Farthest afield from ordinary consideration are Protestant religious orders, usually under Episcopal auspices, offering essentially the same options as are open to Catholics who enter religious orders. There are many kinds of possibilities for supplementary religious experience through the tremendous coverage of religious broadcasting on radio and television, overwhelmingly Protestant in its orientation. Many groups or individuals on the air regularly maintain effective contact with people by mail, evoking even in this apparently impersonal way a very powerful commitment of time and financial support. Other groups, of which Unity is perhaps the most prominent example, are primarily what might be called mail churches; only in quite recent times has this group organized local congregations, and their number is quite small, whereas most people in contact with the group are probably also members of regular denominational churches.[7] Within such churches themselves there are undetermined numbers of possibilities to join with other more highly committed members in groups for prayer, for healing, or for religiously defined psychological encounter on a regular basis and over a sustained period of time.

There are also groups of unconventional believers that gather within the denominational churches, are understood as unconventional forms of expression, and yet do not run in the direction of sectarian division. We present a sampling of several chosen to illustrate the range of options available and also to provide interesting comparisons with other groups described above. The first is an effort sustained for more than two decades but still offering itself as an alternative to the conventional denominations. It is a multidimensional enterprise called the East Harlem Protestant Parish. Begun in 1948 by three young graduates of the most eminent liberal Protestant seminary, Union Theological Seminary in New York City, it

7. See chapter on Unity in Charles Braden, *These Also Believe* (New York: Charles Scribner's Sons, Inc., 1949).

represented an effort to redress an imbalance long apparent in denominational Protestantism: a retreat from the cities to the suburbs and the countryside and the replacement of Protestants by Catholics, Jews, and other non-Protestants.

The East Harlem Protestant Parish began with enthusiasm and gained its experience on the scene, supported by funds from seven different denominations.[8] It has been the prototype for many subsequent efforts, a training ground for many clergy interested in city problems and for many city dwellers neglected by the religious establishment, both Catholic and Protestant. But to this day it is difficult to know whether it has succeeded in generating a significant and continuing response from the people it serves. Why is this the case? It is certainly not for lack of serious intentions, constant self-criticism, and heroic dedication on the part of its leaders. The original leaders were outsiders, as they clearly recognized, and two of the three founders were white in the midst of a black and Puerto Rican population. But they did not want to appear as carpetbaggers, so to speak, so they lived among their people. They took on every social problem from youth gangs and narcotics addiction to broken families, inadequate schools, and the despair of the aging. In the midst of these conditions they experimented valiantly to discover what forms of worship, what methods of education, would bring the saving word of the Christian gospel effectively to the city poor in the decaying brownstones and the crowded housing projects in such a way as to build up among them an organization that could honestly be called a church.

Why did such work not succeed dramatically, once the initial suspicions had been quieted and goodwill demonstrated to people much in need? There are many reasons, but perhaps the best way to suggest them is to draw a comparison between the East Harlem Protestant Parish and the work of John Wesley and his Methodists two centuries previously. Denominational attempts to be effective again in the cities in many ways parallel those of the Wesleyan revival. Well-trained clergymen dismayed by the neglect of the urban poor decide to go among them. The clergymen preach, they open the Scriptures and help the people read, they take their stand against oppression of all varieties in the hope of transforming lives. Many of the basic conditions are the same in both cases, and yet the East

8. For information on the East Harlem Protestant Parish, see Bruce Kenrick, *Come Out of the Wilderness* (New York: Harper and Row, Publishers, Inc., 1962), and George W. Webber, *God's Colony in Man's World* (New York: Abingdon Press, 1960).

Harlem effort, however impressive in many ways, has given no promise of catching fire in the manner of Methodism. Why not?

The comparison with Methodism suggests many possible reasons. In the first place, the founders of the East Harlem Protestant Parish, when they set up their store-front churches and later added to their facilities a church building abandoned by an Italian Pentecostal congregation, did not really move into a religious vacuum. Though the Catholic Church did not minister effectively to its nominal members from a Spanish-speaking background, it was still an important urban presence, unlike the church of Wesley's day. In addition, the store-front church was far from a new thing on city streets, for a walk down almost any one of these streets reveals at least one store-front behind which some Holiness or Pentecostal congregation meets daily and struggles to keep itself together. The kind of emotional intensity that marked the meetings of the early Methodists is palpable at such meetings. It was present too among the families of the East Harlem Protestant Parish, particularly in living room gatherings for prayer and communion, but only as one of several sources if that was what you were looking for.

This kind of spiritual involvement by the people is not all that was sought by the staff of the parish as a response to what they considered the essentials of the faith in the contemporary world. They tended to see the religious problems of the city poor as deeply social problems too, and so they worked to get commitments to political action and social change. To Wesley, and to most evangelists even today, as we have seen, these considerations were secondary to the winning of souls. Changed people were seen as the only reliable basis for meaningful social change.

Certainly this is not a better message than that preached by the theological liberal, and it may even be irresponsible in the modern world, but to take it as a *modus operandi* involves several consequences that may answer our question. A distinctive theological position did not seem to matter to the parish staff. At least it did not matter before they started, but might be worked out as the parish developed. In any case, with seven different denominations as sponsors, the parish could hardly rely on traditional definitions. But Wesley knew what he stood for beforehand, and his willingness to impose his version of the truth on his followers drew out a distinct and committed population of unconventional believers from the common people. Those who refused to listen, who kept committing their sins after refusing the message or who backslid after hearing it sympathetically, were regretfully given up. Such clear drawing of boundaries seems an essential task, especially in the early stages of growth of a distinctive group.

Perhaps it is fair to say of the East Harlem Protestant Parish that the sense of being an unconventional group was realized more obviously in the clergy and other professionals who worked in it than in the people they served. The clergy developed a special sense of what it meant to work in so unconventional a situation and could gain some benefits to apply in their work in more conventional churches. Thus the parish has been widely influential as an example and a prototype for other urban parishes, and it *has* constituted a group of unconventional believers, but of more relevance for religious professionals than for its parishioners.

Interest in the East Harlem experiment seems to have reached a peak for seminarians just before and during the upsurge of civil rights activism in the middle sixties. As we have noted in other connections, the change of direction from civil rights to antiwar activism had important consequences for the redefinition of certain forms of unconventional religious expression. The years of emphasis on inner city work were also years of ecumenical interfaith organizations and general cultural optimism. But when the cities began to burn during the riots, and the war redirected much social criticism, a new and tougher form of social involvement emerged for Protestants who believed that the kingdom of God meant a transformed social order.

In the latter sixties and early seventies such activism often detached itself from connections with local denominational congregations, often from churches altogether. Agencies of the National Council of Churches had worked with migrant farm workers in California and elsewhere, but in doing so they were apt to arouse opposition in local congregations. In most recent years it became more common to find former seminarians working not in churches or innovative parish organizations but in city planning offices or as social workers, even as radical activists. The dynamic Saul Alinsky, himself not a believer, nevertheless became a coworker with groups of church people in organizing the urban poor to agitate for improvement in their living conditions. This kind of activism was new in religious circles, outside of a few hastily suppressed utopian and millennial movements in the late medieval and early Reformation periods. For more established Christian groups the danger of violence tends to be frightening, and the impulse to violence runs too contrary to images of peace to be easily acted upon. In fact, a Christian pacifism such as that of the Quakers is a more familiar phenomenon. It is therefore interesting and significant that in Protestant circles, as well as in Catholic and Jewish ones to a lesser degree, the interest in social action first articulated in the Social Gospel movement of the turn of the century, and later expressed in such efforts as the East Harlem Protestant Parish, turned more radical in the later sixties.

ACTIVISM AND SECULAR MONASTICISM

Probably the best example of this change of direction is an organization comparable to the East Harlem Protestant Parish in many ways, but in many ways also significantly different. It is a very active group centered in Chicago and is called the Ecumenical Institute. The headquarters of the institute is in Chicago largely as a result of the fact that the second postwar gathering of the World Council of Churches took place in nearby Evanston in 1954 and helped to focus an interest in ecumenism. Thus the Ecumenical Institute came into being in the latter fifties as a division of the Church Federation of Greater Chicago, and in later years it extended its work into the worldwide arena.[9] At times its leaders were reported to be in conversation with Vatican officials, naturally in the aftermath of Vatican II. Such a mode of operation is not unusual in the context of the major trends of twentieth-century Protestantism, and if this were all the Ecumenical Institute did, it would probably not qualify as a group of unconventional believers in our sense.

But conventional ecumenical activity has hardly been the main emphasis of the institute, especially since the direction of its efforts came into the hands of a man named Joseph W. Mathews in 1962. Mathews is a clergyman of the Methodist Church, as by now we might expect. During the Second World War he was a chaplain in the Army, then a teacher of Christian ethics first at Colgate and later at Southern Methodist University in Dallas. In 1956 he became director of studies at the Faith-and-Life Community in Austin, Texas, site of the state university, his last post before moving the institution to Chicago. Mathews is therefore by long experience a specialist in adult education in Christianity. Faith-and-Life was an appropriately ecumenical tradition, but in Chicago Mathews had an opportunity to broaden its scope and, more to the point, to organize the Ecumenical Institute into a new kind of church, one that would

9. Literature on the Ecumenical Institute is not extensive. Information given here is derived from *IE*, journal of the movement, an article from *The New York Times* on the institute by Edward Fiske, and a personal visit to the New York group.

serve as an ecclesiastical action group and, more recently, an agency for no less than "the reconstruction of society and the resurgence of humanness." [10]

The basis for broadening its scope has been a highly structured educational program and, no less importantly, a dedicated group of people prepared to make highly unusual efforts to communicate it. One element in this system is a kind of military imagery, possibly a legacy of Mathews' military experience and a curious reminiscence of the Salvation Army. The institute trains clergy to be a "cadre" for the renewal effort, and in the process subjects them to a tight corporate discipline. In 1964 it leased the campus of Bethany, a former Church of the Brethren seminary located in an area of Western Chicago surrounded by a black community. Now it was possible to maintain a unified community, and the people who took up residence there, both clergy and laity, came to consider themselves committed to a kind of contemporary Protestant monasticism.

The life style developed in Chicago became the model for outpost groups in other cities. Membership includes families as well as single people, but the discipline sounds some echoes of ancient monastic life. Each group is divided into subgroups that take responsibility for all their members. At the start of the common supper each group reports on the whereabouts of any member not present. All rise at dawn or before and celebrate in a liturgy of song and prayer. Adults afterward go to their various jobs, either in teaching for the institute or in secular employment. Income is pooled and standard stipends paid to all. Children are cared for communally, and meals for those in residence are eaten in common.

This monasticism, by contrast to the older kind, sees no reason for isolation from the world. In fact, to become isolated as a group would be a betrayal of the institute's purposes. From the start it plunged itself into deep engagement with its world on two main fronts—the black community of the immediate neighborhood and the faltering denominational churches of the rest of America; in later years it even became international in scope, trying to put into effect the idealistic missionary intentions of its Protestant predecessors early in the century. The local efforts concentrated on helping black people lose their "victim" image of themselves. Work in churches involved the teaching of a highly developed set of courses divided into two series—religious studies (RS-I and so forth) and cultural studies (CS-I and its successors). The distinctive contribu-

10. *IE*, VIII,5, September 10, 1972.

tion of the institute was that religious life has to be just as dedicated and disciplined as life in the monastery, but that it also has to be lived out in the here-and-now. You do not reach an understanding of religion in your own time apart from an equally profound search for the meaning (or lack of meaning) in modern culture. It is a challenging argument.

Thus far the results are mixed. Ecumenical Institute people spent a lot of mental effort forming models for understanding modern culture in a comprehensive way, but their critics replied that many of the basic assumptions of the plans were shaky and yet were not allowed to be questioned. Members of the institute took up "studies in revolutionary maneuvers," set up a "strategy front," and armed it with a "book arsenal" that included works by Hans Küng and other members of the intellectual avant-garde, if the image is appropriate, of post-Vatican II European Catholicism. In this revolutionary frame of mind their newsletter published radical models for the church and even, as early as 1967, spoke of what "the new woman" would be like.[11] The institute tried to set up a local "congregational covenant group" of churches in their Chicago environs, but there is little evidence these churches were willing to follow so definite a lead. Then in 1968 the revolutionary rhetoric bore bitter fruit in the riots following the assassination of the Reverend Martin Luther King, Jr. The institute's buildings were marked for burning by local militants, and fires were actually started during Holy Week. It was not easy to turn them into celebration. What was being called the Fifth City, in reference to the area in which the institute was located, no longer seemed so easy to identify with local aspirations.

It may be said that the first decade of teaching in the Chicago institute concentrated on tactics, on ways of getting the message across and enlisting highly committed teachers who could do that with single-minded devotion. The jargon of the lessons is distinctive, the model-building a relentless intellectual exercise that is supposed always to be applied to social reality. The single-mindedness offended denominational liberals for whom nothing is ever that clear; the so-called evangelicals were also offended for the opposite reason, that the method was always being applied to structures but did not seem adequate to personal salvation, to the deep inwardness that is the goal of much unconventional belief. Perhaps in answer to this difficulty, in the year of the fires the institute was also being called the Spirit Movement and was going international. More to the

11. *IE*, 3.3, January 1967.

point, by 1972 Mathews, now turning sixty, recognized a need to redirect the movement after 20 years of church renewal to the global goal previously mentioned—the reconstruction of society. This too is seen as a 20-year task, and it bears a rather remarkable resemblance to the slogan "evangelization of world in our generation," which was the motto of a previous mission movement among Protestants: the Student Volunteer Movement of the generation prior to the First World War.[12]

Another motto from the ecumenical movement proper, the great effort that culminated in the formation of the World Council of Churches a quarter of a century ago, also has a curious ring to it in the context of its rather unusual offspring, the Ecumenical Institute. One of the constituent units of the World Council was an organization called "Life and Work," which took an ethical rather than a theological approach to the problem of church union on the theory that "dogma divides, service unites." [13] The activism of the Ecumenical Institute has proved that this slogan too is rather hollow, for service unites only when it operates within certain social conventions; when those conventions change, conflict results. On many mission fields the social benevolence of Western missionaries is often now unwelcome, as the institute's work seemed also to appear to some of its Chicago neighbors. Needless to say, the work to revitalize local churches is at least an indirect affront to those who have been working in them. Serious service work, therefore, can be divisive too.

Some other comparisons suggest themselves. Some have remarked on the great personal influence of Joseph Mathews as a model for the teaching style of many of the institute's workers; in this sense they have compared him and his movement with Frank Buchman and Moral Re-Armament, as previously mentioned. In a somewhat apologetic tone one might also draw a comparison between the Ecumenical Institute and Scientology—apologetically because the institute has never been controversial in quite the same way as Scientology, nor Mathews' credibility under such deep suspicion as Ron Hubbard's. Yet there are some similarities in the movements—in the wholehearted commitment to a contemporary technological jargon, the extraordinary dedication of the workers to a particular method as well as to a particular way of thinking, and a powerful optimism about the ability of a highly trained elite corps of workers

12. H. Shelton Smith, Robert T. Handy, and Lefferts A. Loetscher, eds., *American Christianity* (New York: Charles Scribner's Sons, Inc., 1960), Vol. 2, pp. 566ff.

13. *Ibid.*, pp. 567–69.

to make global changes. It is curious but true that in the light of this comparison Ron Hubbard's predictions seem the more modest of the two. But when these two contemporaries no longer are capable of leadership, can their movements retain their vitality?

NEW LIFE IN OLDER FORMS

It would not do to leave the impression here, in a discussion of unconventional forms of belief in the more traditional denominations, that only extraordinary efforts like the East Harlem Protestant Parish or the Ecumenical Institute carry the quality of authenticity and more than usual commitment. As in other faiths, the efforts of many deeply committed people combine into groups in varieties of ways and on many occasions to take them beyond conventional religious experience. It is not only in cities, for example, that creative Protestant ministries have tried to answer, or perhaps to create, the need for unconventional groups in the midst of the main-line churches. Are we also able to find the unconventional in unexpected places?

In answer let it be said that in the age of Freud it would seem that the old legacy of rational religion would be one of the least vital religious traditions. Yet this is not so, and in recent years one of the most interesting examples of new growth and vitality can be found within what is now the Unitarian-Universalist Association. The groups so combined in 1961 go back to the late eighteenth and early nineteenth centuries. They rejected the dominant trends of evangelical Protestantism, both the radical sinfulness of Calvinist doctrine and the radical salvationism, if we may use such a word, of the revival. Both churches in their own way believed in a benevolent and reasonable God and required no extraordinary responses on the part of their members. They well suited certain New England temperaments, but they also won adherents among liberated personalities of the frontier towns. In more recent years they have been mostly quiet, middle-class associations.

Yet in the postwar era, especially in the Unitarian wing of the church, a movement began that centered in what were called Unitarian fellowships and grew until there were twice as many or more of them as there were Unitarian churches. Unitarianism is a faith of "unbelief," or at least opposition to most of the dogmas and the seeming irrationality of traditional Christianity. In a way this opposition provides a good basis for organization, especially, as it turns out, for the fellowship sort of organization.[14] Clergy and church buildings are somewhat uneasy aspects of the faith of Unitarians; the fellowships are led by laypeople. There is a diversity of beliefs, and God for many members is more an abstract concept than a personal being. Most members, it is said, would not call themselves Christians.

Why, then, do they form groups and assume the look of dynamic growth? Because, as one writer says, they "join an approach, not a creed." [15] They find good companionship in their criticism of received ideas and systems of authority. They welcome, on the one hand, any who find repugnant the emotionalism or the dogmatism of more authoritarian churches, or, on the other, the hypocrisy of people who claim to follow those old traditions but do not act as though they did. Unitarians are honest people, and perhaps not overly expressive in their feelings, but like other unconventional believers they are united into groups by the sense that theirs is a distinctive faith. In its own way, this too is a deep commitment.

14. For information on Unitarian fellowships, see Laile E. Bartlett, *Bright Galaxy* (Boston: Beacon Press, 1960).

15. Laile E. Bartlett, "The Structuring of Unbelief," unpublished paper.

Youth and the Future
of Unconventional Belief

The concluding pages of the introductory chapter of this work carry a contemporary student's description of how the quest for living religious experience can become a matter of life and death. Not all the groups we have looked at in the intervening pages deserve to be taken that seriously; yet we have maintained that they are almost all examples of unconventional religion. Does this mean that some are less authentic, less worthy because their adherents seemingly believe in them less ardently? No, because in many cases unconventional believers are not as articulate, and not as ready to reveal themselves, as the student whose writing was reproduced there. Yet you can still raise an argument by criticizing the principles of Christian Science to one of its believers. Even should you attack the rationality of a Unitarian in some cases, the response will be a clear indication that the belief, the allegiance of the person in question to a point of view, is a matter of the intense commitment of an unconventional believer.

But it may still be true that there is a qualitative difference between the student's personal vision and the religious groups we have described, all of which are a part of the familiar context of American religious traditions. Does the student signal the dawn of a new age? It has been a commonplace in recent years to speak of a "counter-culture" that has defined itself by opposition to the conventional cultural and religious values. It is obvious that one aspect of this movement has been the formation of a considerable number of communal religious groups, many of which place religious values at the center of their programs. Such groups were very numerous during the nineteenth century,[1] so that their presence is not a novelty in American society. But if the quality of the new groups is somehow unprecedented, if they provide a model for Americans to emulate in future years, and particularly if those involved may themselves expect what is gained from present membership to be carried forward into their adulthood, then we may rejoice that a sensitive individual's insights may indeed be the signal that in the new generation we have an unusually precious social resource. Does the counterculture offer this to America?

One may hope that it does, but the evidence is mixed. It is by no means always the case that the formation of groups of young people on a religious basis has resulted in such a sense of peace and harmony as is the case with the best of them. It is not within the scope of this book to sort out the variety of traditions and innovations expressed by all the new groups, particularly the derivatives from Eastern religious traditions,[2] or even the Christian groups called Jesus People, who are receiving detailed attention in other works.[3] But since the last do relate closely to groups we have examined here, it is relevant to ask in what respects they provide answers to the questions asked above.

It is apparent that many of the Jesus People are strictly traditionalists in doctrinal matters, as literal in their use of the Scriptures as any fundamentalists.[4] Thus in all essential respects they can be compared with unconventional groups of the past. When this is done there is little to differentiate them as new or progressive. In fact, most of them would probably not wish to be thought of in those terms. In addition, the groups of Jesus People are in many cases coercive rather than liberating. One of the sadder religious news stories of 1973 was a series of items about the efforts of parents to

1. For a first-hand account of many of these groups see Charles Nordhoff, *The Communistic Societies of the United States,* originally published in 1875 and recently reprinted (New York: Schocken Books Inc., 1965).

2. See Jacob Needleman, *The New Religions* (Garden City, N. Y.: Doubleday and Company, Inc., 1970) and Robert S. Ellwood, Jr., *Religious and Spiritual Groups in Modern America* (Englewood Cliffs, N. J.: Prentice-Hall., 1973).

3. On Jesus People see Robert S. Ellwood, Jr., *One Way: The Jesus Movement and Its Meaning* (Englewood Cliffs, N.J.: Prentice-Hall, Inc., 1973).

4. Good illustrations of the fundamentalism of some Jesus People are provided by Mary White Harder, James T. Richardson, and Robert B. Simmonds in "Jesus People," *Psychology Today* (December, 1972), 45ff.

recover, or more literally, to recapture their children from some such groups, through abductions and a thoroughgoing "de-programming." [5] This was done by means of the contrary use of the same biblical evidence that had been the intellectual basis for their life in the religious commune. Stories of terribly painful family conflicts over young people's participation in various groups had indeed surfaced in prior years as well.[6] The young people in many cases vigorously resisted being returned home. This may be a commentary either on the quality of family life or on the capacity of the Christian faith still to generate ardent commitment. It is not, however, evidence of anything radically new or particularly hopeful for the future of American society when the present generation matures.

What is also not new, but what *is* distinctive about youthful participation in religious groups, is that it tends to be intensely felt, and that this intensity is commonly expressed in exclusive and even cruel loyalties. Those familiar with the writings of Erik Erikson may invoke at this point his ideas about the formation and maintenance of identity.[7] But it is surely no secret that the achievement of adult identity often involves defense against attachment to parents as well as flight from chaos, indifference, and what might be called the moral desert-places. Thus the apprehension that the issue of life and death hangs in the balance on the basis of an either-or religious choice tends to be related to youthful groups rather than to groups of older people. Although older people too are deeply concerned with religious meaning, for young people it is the boundaries of the group that must be defended. Perhaps when one does not yet know the boundaries of his own personality, the anxiety about being unsure of himself changes to anger when attacks are directed against the group to which he is committed and by which he has been affirmed.

The point is that an obvious emotional intensity and even rigidity should not be thought of as the necessary marks of participation in groups of unconventional believers. Religion organizes many aspects of life, and many interests can provide the basis for extraordinary degrees of religious participation. The results are often colorful, sometimes inspiring, and sometimes exasperating for their exposure of apparent weakness, gullibility, or a premature refusal to answer questions that to the forthright mind need to be squarely

5. See articles on Ted Patrick and his "de-programming" of Jesus People in New York City and the national press in the spring of 1973.

6. See for example an article in *The New York Times* datelined November 24, 1971, entitled "Ill Winds Buffet a Communal Sect of Young Fundamentalists."

7. Erik H. Erikson, *Identity: Youth and Crisis* (New York: W. W. Norton and Company, Inc., 1968).

faced. Do the unconventional believers, therefore, have nothing to say to conventional believers? I do not think so, for all of us have our inadequacies and share a need to commit ourselves to answers for ultimate questions that in principle cannot be answered. In such matters even what seems a foolish answer may earn our admiration. In an age when popular entertainment has brought back the pathetically gallant figure of Don Quixote, surely the unconventional believer, whatever his intentions, can be respected for his suggestion to the conventionally religious person that his dreams too might be richer if they were impossible—richer, and conceivably also more productive for waking life.

SOME NOTES ON METHOD

If some recognizable degree of intensity is not a characteristic mark of the unconventional believer and the unconventional religious group, what is? Can any general statements be made about the disparate collection of religious groups described in previous chapters? If a deeply felt emotional intensity about the identity of the group, and by extension that of its members, tends to be associated with the unconventional groups whose members are mostly young people, other characteristics may be singled out as distinguishing features of differently constituted groups. The problem is to assemble those characteristics in a coherent form that summarizes and explains how unconventional groups differ from conventional ones.

Briefly, the criterion on which the selection of groups of unconventional believers is based starts with the proposition that religious groups of any kind are founded on the need for authoritative direction of human life. When the source or sources of such direction have origins that are understood to stand beyond sensory evidence, the source typically is regarded as divine and the basis for religious responses. A religious group is a kind of consensus that the source and process of direction should be symbolized in a particular way. What distinguishes the unconventional from the conventional believer is a matter of degree. In whatever way the authority of faith is symbolized in a particular religious tradition, the unconventional believer takes that authority more seriously, and makes it more central to the way he leads his life, than the conventional believer does.

There is, to be sure, considerable variety in unconventional responses. Emotional intensity is a factor in some of them. If for your group it is necessary to be born again, then your rebirth must go to the roots of spiritual identity. If adherence to the truth of the Scriptures is the main canon of your group's faith, then you will study the Scriptures and use them more than many others do. Sometimes the primary symbol is not the words of the Scriptures or a creed, but a gesture or a visual sign. At one point in the history of the Russian Orthodox Church, for example, people were willing to stake their lives on the issue of whether the sign of blessing should be given with two fingers or with three.[8]

This kind of devotion is uncommon in the traditions represented in the religious groups of America, but it is an example of the kind of loyalty to particular symbols that may inspire what seems to the conventional believer an irrational response. Most groups, of course, do not base their faith on the identity of a single symbol but on a complex set of images, verbal formulations, official roles of authority, patterns of feeling, and codes of behavior. What is emphasized in any particular group is the starting point for the unconventional believer's quest for a satisfactory experience of faith. He may find satisfaction in some of the possibilities offered by the group he already belongs to, but if not, he must seek it elsewhere, either in a group already in being or in a group that he himself creates if circumstances permit. In the new group some new combination of symbols and structural features will be proclaimed as the answer to the unconventional need.

The distinction between conventional and unconventional in religion, finally, is like the distinction between the old and the new morality. Each depends for its meaning on the other, and each in a way requires the other if either is to be adequately understood. The study of groups of unconventional believers is important because such groups give us glimpses into the future of religion generally, but more importantly, because without such study the conventional believer does not fully know what he is committed to and does not ask with full awareness even the religious questions of his own tradition. One final point may be made in defense of the unconventional believers. You cannot meet the people involved in such groups without usually being struck by a wholly estimable solidity of character. To keep members of such groups at a distance and call them absurd or crazy is to cheapen your own humanity. Their ways may not appeal to you, but they win the gift of your respect, and in the wilderness of much contemporary existence, that is something worth giving.

8. See James H. Nichols, *History of Christianity 1650–1950* (New York: The Ronald Press, 1956), pp. 22–23.

Index